JOURNAL FOR THE STUDY OF THE NEW TESTAMENT SUPPLEMENT SERIES
137

Executive Editor
Stanley E. Porter

Sheffield Academic Press

The Graeco-Roman Context
of Early Christian Literature

Roman Garrison

Journal for the Study of the New Testament
Supplement Series 137

While research and writing are fulfilling and rewarding, life itself is a joy because of Evann, Jessica, and John, to whom this work is dedicated.

Published by Sheffield Academic Press Ltd
Mansion House
19 Kingfield Road
Sheffield S11 9AS
England

Printed on acid-free paper in Great Britain
by Bookcraft Ltd
Midsomer Norton, Bath

British Library Cataloguing in Publication Data

A catalogue record for this book is available
from the British Library

ISBN 1-85075-646-5

CONTENTS

ABBREVIATIONS

AB	Anchor Bible
CBQ	*Catholic Biblical Quarterly*
CP	*Classical Philology*
ETL	*Ephemerides theologicae lovanienses*
HTR	*Harvard Theological Review*
Int	*Interpretation*
JAAR	*Journal of the American Academy of Religion*
JBL	*Journal of Biblical Literature*
JSNTSup	*Journal for the Study of the New Testament*, Supplement Series
JTS	*Journal of Theological Studies*
NovT	*Novum Testamentum*
NTS	*New Testament Studies*
PerRS	*Perspectives in Religious Studies*
SR	*Studies in Religion/Sciences religieuses*
TDNT	G. Kittel and G. Friedrich (eds.), *Theological Dictionary of the New Testament*
ZNW	*Zeitschrift für die neutestamentliche Wissenschaft*

Chapter 1

THE GRAECO-ROMAN CONTEXT OF EARLY CHRISTIANITY

Introduction

The church today battles with the corrosive acids of contemporary culture; yet the language and images of the day (or the hour) are often employed by the church in order to make the gospel message more 'understandable' to the members of that same contemporary culture. Consequently, a strange and strained relationship has developed between Christianity and modern Western society. This problem has an ancient history.

The Negative View of Graeco-Roman Mythology

Early Christianity firmly rejected Graeco-Roman traditions about the gods, and the contemporary society regarded the Christians as a threat to popular conventions derived from mythology. It is claimed that when he was brought out for execution and the herald announced, 'Polycarp has confessed that he is a Christian', the crowd of Gentiles and Jews (ἐθνῶν τε καὶ Ἰουδαίων) cried out for his death, accusing him of being 'the destroyer of our gods' (ὁ τῶν ἡμετέρων θεῶν καθαιρέτης).[1] The historical accuracy of this report is not of central concern; rather our interest is drawn to the author's suggestion that Christianity was a danger both to the gods of the Graeco-Roman religions and even to the god of the Jews.

Similarly, in his apologetic letter to Diognetus, the writer praises his reader's interest:

> ...you are exceedingly zealous to learn the religion of the Christians and are asking very clear and careful questions concerning them...who is the god in whom they believe and how they worship him... [For the

1. *Mart. Pol.* 12.1-2.

Christians] do not reckon as gods those who are considered to be so by the Greeks, nor keep the superstition of the Jews...[2]

Again the clear implication is that Christianity's distinctive set of beliefs rejects, indeed repudiates, certain features of both Greek and Jewish religions.

As the gospel message spread through the Empire, early Christianity found the Zeus-traditions to be repugnant and the God of the Hebrew scriptures in extreme need of reformation.[3] The consequent theological reconstruction project required the complete removal of many ideas within the Graeco-Roman thought-world and attempts to remodel and restore the traditions about Yahweh. Our principal concern here is with the former.

Several writers in early Christianity mock or ridicule the popular mythology of the Graeco-Roman culture and its implications for the theology of that world. This criticism is perhaps most emphatic in Tatian.[4] There is as well reference to the tragic effect of the myths on the morality of those who hear such stories. Justin maintains that these tales were designed to corrupt the young who mistakenly believe it to be their duty to imitate the character of the gods.[5]

Clement of Alexandria rebukes the 'atheism' of the Greek myths, deploring their crude, even blasphemous, anthropomorphisms, and rejoices that Plato among many philosophers embraced the truth, declaring 'the one and only true God to be God'.[6]

Prominent in Plato's *Republic*,[7] this criticism of mythology is not peculiar to Christianity but is indeed a feature of Greek thought at least as early as Xenophanes and Heracleitus.[8] While Plato, however, was

---

2. *Diogn.* 1; cf. 8.1; Ignatius, *Magn.* 8.1; 10.3; Ignatius, *Phld.* 6.1; *Barn.* 4.7-8; *2 Clem.* 2.3: '[the Jews] seemed to have God.'

3. The significance of Marcion warrants attention but cannot be the focus of this discussion. Cf. A.C. McGiffert, *The God of the Early Christians* (New York: Charles Scribner's Sons, 1924): '...conversion to Christianity did not necessarily carry with it the acceptance of the God of the Jews' (p. 66).

4. J. Daniélou, *Gospel Message and Hellenistic Culture* (Philadelphia: Westminster, 1973), p. 75.

5. *Apology* 21; cf. Epictetus, *Discourses* 2.14.11-13. See also Tatian, *Address to the Greeks* 10; Philostratus, *Life of Apollonius of Tyana* 5.14.

6. *Exhortation to the Greeks* 4; 6.

7. 377C-391E.

8. Sextus Empiricus, *Against the Mathematicians* 1.289; 9.193. See also Pythagoras's reported attitude in Diogenes Laertius 8.21. Cf. W. Jaeger, *Early*

concerned with the political/social influence of such views of the gods,[9] several others were critical of what they perceived to be 'bad theology'. A more personal statement of the problem is found in the second-century satirist Lucian who expresses his own anxiety in trying to understand the myths about the gods:

> While I was a boy, when I read in Homer and Hesiod about wars and quarrels, not only of the demigods but of the gods themselves, and besides about their amours and assaults and abductions and lawsuits and banishing fathers and marrying sisters, I thought that all these things were right, and I felt an uncommon impulsion toward them.

> But when I came of age, I found that the laws contradicted the poets and forbade adultery, quarreling, and theft. So I was plunged into great uncertainty, not knowing how to deal with my own case. For the gods would never have committed adultery and quarreled with each other, I thought, unless they deemed these actions right, and the lawgivers would not recommend the opposite course unless they supposed it to be advantageous. Since I was in a dilemma, I resolved to go to the men whom they call philosophers...begging them to deal with me as they would, and to show me a plain, solid path in life.[10]

The apostle Paul describes his own parallel 'maturing' with a similar construction: 'When I was a child, I spoke like a child, I thought like a child, I reasoned like a child; when I became an adult, I put an end to childish ways' (1 Cor. 13.11). Was Paul acknowledging that as he 'grew' in faith and knowledge it was necessary to abandon ideas that had once shaped his character?

The most significant myth about God that Plato repudiated was the idea that God was a source of deception.[11] Plato insisted God that had no motive for wanting to deceive and that Homer was to be censured for claiming that Zeus sent a 'lying dream' to Agamemnon.[12]

Christianity and Greek Paideia (Cambridge: Belknap, 1961), p. 28: 'Disbelief in the gods of the old poets and the popular religion was as old as philosophy itself'; and pp. 48-49. Cf. also, A.H. Armstrong and R.A. Markus, *Christian Faith and Greek Philosophy* (New York: Sheed & Ward, 1960), p. 2; T. Irwin, *Classical Thought* (Oxford: Oxford University Press, 1989), p. 38.

9. Cf. *Euthyphro* 6A-B.

10. *Menippus* 3 (trans. A.M. Harmon). Cf. Daniélou, *Gospel Message*, p. 16.

11. Interestingly, Clement of Alexandria describes Plato as 'truth-loving', *Strom.* 1.8.

12. *Republic* 382E-383A, commenting on *Iliad* 2.1-41. Suetonius reports that the emperor Caligula considered having the works of Homer destroyed because he

Early Christianity came to embrace this Platonic theology, even affirming the *impossibility* of God's lying.[13] This is at least a modification, perhaps a repudiation, of the view of God found in the Hebrew scripture, including a passage which is eerily parallel to the *Iliad* story rejected by Plato:

> Then Micaiah said, 'Therefore hear the word of the Lord: I saw the Lord sitting on his throne, with all the host of heaven standing beside him to the left and to the right of him. And the Lord said, "Who will entice Ahab, so that he may go up and fall at Ramoth-gilead?" Then one said one thing, and another said another, until a spirit came forward and stood before the Lord, saying, "I will entice him."
>
> "How?" the Lord asked him. He replied, "I will go out and be a lying spirit in the mouth of all his prophets." Then the Lord said, "You are to entice him, and you shall succeed; go out and do it." So you see, the Lord has put a lying spirit in the mouth of all these your prophets; the Lord has decreed disaster for you' (1 Kgs 22.19-23; cf. 2 Chron. 18.18-22).

Did early Christianity 'mature' in its understanding of God? Was there a willingness to give up 'childish' perceptions? Does the theology of early Christianity exhibit an apparent development consistent with Plato's programme of demythologizing?[14] These issues provide a framework for understanding the harsh contrast in John's Gospel between Jesus who is the 'Truth' and the devil who is regarded as 'the father of lies' and suggests the author's ambivalence towards the character of Pontius Pilate which is suggested by the latter's sophistic question 'What is truth?' (18.38).

The 'true' God is also a theme in Paul's letters. In referring to the conversion of the Thessalonian Christians, the apostle speaks of their having 'turned from idols to the true and living God' (1 Thess. 1.9). The term 'living', describing God, is fairly common in the Hebrew scripture (e.g., Deut. 5.26; 1 Sam. 17.26; Ps. 42.2; 84.2; Isa. 37.4, 17). The designation of God as '*true* and living', however, is clearly intended to offer a sharp contrast to the character of idols who are by implication false[15]

wanted the same privilege as Plato in excluding Homer from his society, *Gaius Caligula* 34.

13. Cf. Tit. 1.2; Heb. 6:18; *Herm. Man.* 10.3; *Mart. Pol.* 14.2; Ignatius, *Rom.* 8.2; *1 Clem.* 27.2. Plato uses the term ἀδύνατον in *Republic* 381C. Cf. *Apology* 21B.

14. Cf. *Herm. Man.* 3.2.

15. Cf. Justin, *Apology* 6: 'We do proclaim ourselves atheists as regards those whom you call gods, but not with respect to the Most, True God...'

and dead.[16] This is already evident in the only passage in the Hebrew Bible to use the adjectives 'true and living' of God:

> But the Lord is the true God; he is the living God and the everlasting King (Jer. 10.10).

This passage is part of a poem 'urging the people not to adopt the religion of the heathen or worship their gods'.[17] Idols are only false gods made of 'dead' stone, wood, or metal: 'there is no breath in them' (cf. 10.1-5, 8, 14-15).

While it is undeniable that Paul regarded the Thessalonians' former objects of worship to be lifeless, the incident recorded in Acts 14.8-18 raises the possibility that 'living' in 1 Thess. 1.8 may be a virtual taunt, not only of the gods in general but of the god who had, according to mythology, died—Zeus himself.[18]

In Acts 14 Paul and Barnabas are regarded as gods in human form and the priest of Zeus prepares to offer sacrifices in their honour. In horror Paul calls out, 'Why are you doing this?...Turn from these worthless things to the living God...' (14.11-15). A deliberate contrast may be implied between Zeus and the living God.[19] Here again the apparent lament of Lucian offers a significant parallel:

> Why shouldn't I hear thunder Timocles? But whether it is Zeus that thunders or not you no doubt know best, coming as you do from some place or other where the gods live! However, the people who come here from Crete tell us a different tale, that a grave is pointed out there with a tombstone standing upon it which proves that Zeus cannot thunder anymore, as he has been dead this long time.[20]

> As for the Cretans, they not only say that Zeus was born and brought up among them, but even point out his tomb. We were mistaken all this while, then, in thinking that thunder and rain and everything else comes from Zeus. If we had only known—he has been dead and buried in Crete all the time![21]

---

16. Cf. *2 Clem.* 3.1.

17. J. Bright, *Jeremiah* (AB, 21; Garden City, NY: Doubleday, 1965), p. 79.

18. See A.B. Cook, *Zeus* (New York: Biblo & Tannen, 1964), p. 157.

19. Cf. C. Breytenbach, 'Zeus und der Lebendige Gott', *NTS* 39 (1993), pp. 396-413.

20. Lucian, *Zeus Rants* 45.

21. Lucian, *On Sacrifices* 10. For the Cretan context of the legend see W.K.C. Guthrie, *The Greeks and their Gods* (Boston: Beacon Press, 1951), pp. 50-51. Other relevant texts include Callimachus, *Hymn to Zeus* lines 8ff. (cf. Tit. 1.12!); Theophilus,

In 1 Thessalonians Paul may be alluding to that community's having turned from the false, lifeless idols represented by the 'dead' Zeus to the living and true God, the Father of Jesus Christ.

Early Christianity ridiculed the religion and gods of the Graeco-Roman culture. There was, however, much in the literature of that world that was appropriated by the church for the purposes of furthering the gospel.

The Positive View of 'Other Voices'

Early Christianity exhibited a cautious acceptance of the Greek poets and philosophers. There seems to have been a 'Balaam's ass' attitude: according to ancient Hebrew tradition, when Israel, in moving towards the land of the covenant, set up camp in the plains of Moab, the king of that region, Balak, sought divine protection for his own people against these invaders. He sent messengers to a prophet (or holy man) named Balaam asking him to damn the Israelites. We read the king's words in Num. 22.5-6:

> A people has come out of Egypt; they have spread over the face of the earth, and they have settled next to me. Come now, curse this people for me, since they are stronger than I; perhaps I shall be able to defeat them and drive them from the land. For I know that whomever you bless is blessed, and whomever you curse is cursed.

After initial reluctance even to accompany the messengers in returning to the king, Balaam finally agrees to come to him but only after God says, 'If the men have come to summon you, get up and go with them; but do only what I tell you to do.' Strangely God is angered by Balaam's decision and an angel of Yahweh with a sword blocks his path as he travels. But this supernatural creature is invisible to Balaam. Only his donkey can see the angel and the beast resists his rider's promptings. Balaam becomes furious with the donkey and beats the animal viciously. The tradition then reports that the donkey's mouth was opened by Yahweh and it said, 'What have I done to you, that you have struck me these three times?' It is remarkable that Balaam carries on a quite reasonable, if heated, conversation with the animal.

Ad Autolycum 1.10; Lucian, *The Patriot* 10; Cicero, *de nat. deor.* 3.53; Tatian, *or. adv. Graec.* 27; Clement of Alexandria, *Protr.* 2.37.4; Chrysostom, *Ep. Paul ad Tit.* 3. See also Tertullian, *Apology* 12.5.

This story is not only interesting; it is not merely ancient. The tradition has been embraced by the Jewish and Christian faiths as sacred scripture, as being in some sense the word of God. And as such there is speculation about the purpose of God in this revelation. Undoubtedly, the principal emphasis of the whole narrative is on Israel's privileged calling and irrevocable blessing as a partner in the covenant; but this subplot concerning Balaam and his donkey captures the imagination and amuses the reader. In a dramatic manner, this minor part of the tradition seems to foreshadow or perhaps illustrate the early Christian attitude towards the Graeco-Roman poets and philosophers.

In the early church there is the belief that the authorities of Graeco-Roman thought are like dumb animals, senseless and of little value, often opposed to those who would proclaim God's word. Yet some early Christian authors, even some whose writings are now regarded by many as sacred scripture, acknowledge that the Graeco-Roman poets and philosophers are other voices, tongues sometimes loosed by God that on occasion have spoken the truth. Some even referred to this process as an act of divine inspiration; as the authors of scripture were moved by God, so were these voices of Graeco-Roman thought.[22]

The New Testament
Paul is a striking example of this contradictory or paradoxical attitude. In his first extant letter to the Corinthians, the apostle mocks so-called human wisdom, insisting that it is unwilling, indeed unable, to embrace the apparently absurd message of the crucified messiah. He writes in 1.20-21:

> Where is the one who is wise? Where is the scribe? Where is the debater of this age? Has not God made foolish the wisdom of the world? For since, in the wisdom of God, the world did not know God through wisdom, God decided, through the foolishness of our proclamation, to save those who believe.

This hostility is echoed in Colossians[23] and throughout early Christian literature and is most pronounced in Tertullian.[24] Yet despite this initially harsh judgment of 'worldly wisdom', Paul later *in the same letter* quotes

22. Cf. Clement of Alexandria, *Exhortation to the Greeks* 6; Daniélou, *Gospel Message*, pp. 40, 54-55.

23. Cf. Origen's comment on Col. 2.8 in *Against Celsus*, the preface; Tertullian, *Prescription against Heretics* 7.

24. *Apology* 46: '...where is there any likeness between the Christian and the philosopher? between the disciple of Greece and of heaven?'

Menander with approval (15.33): 'Do not be deceived: "Bad company ruins good morals."'[25]

Elsewhere the New Testament portrays Paul as quite sympathetic to these other voices of truth, the Graeco-Roman poets and philosophers. In Acts 17.28, Paul tells his Athenian audience:

> For 'in him we live and move and have our being,' as even some of your poets have said, 'For we are indeed his offspring.'

Here the apostle is represented as quoting both Epimenides and Aratus.[26] Epimenides is again cited in Tit. 1.12 where the Cretan poet/philosopher is designated as a προφήτης:

> One of themselves, a prophet of their own, said, 'Cretans are always liars, evil beasts, lazy gluttons.'

The one who is himself a beast is given the voice of truth![27] One might be inclined to ask how someone who always lies can tell the truth, but that cannot be pursued here. It is more significant that the author of Titus regards Epimenides as a legitimate authority to be cited in the cause of condemning the people of Crete.[28]

Thus the New Testament promotes two distinct attitudes to the Graeco-Roman poets and philosophers: (1) a rejection of sources outside the 'biblical'[29] tradition as ungodly and spiritually bankrupt; (2) an acceptance of sources outside the 'biblical' tradition that affirm the author's doctrine. This tension characterizes the continuing early Christian perspectives on these other voices.

---

25. Cf. Menander, *Thais* 218. In this context it would be vital to consider Paul's relationship to contemporary moral philosophy and to Hellenistic standards of rhetoric and exhortation. See among the many possible sources: F.W. Danker, 'Menander and the New Testament', *NTS* 10 (1964), pp. 365-68; A.J. Malherbe, *Paul and the Popular Philosophers* (Philadelphia: Fortress Press, 1989); W.A. Meeks, *The Moral World of the First Christians* (Philadelphia: Westminster, 1986); and C. Forbes, 'Comparison, Self-Praise and Irony: Paul's Boasting and the Conventions of Hellenistic Rhetoric', *NTS* 32 (1986), pp. 1-30.

26. G.H.C. Macgregor, *Acts* (Interpreter's Bible, 9; New York: Abingdon, 1954), p. 236.

27. 'That testimony is true', Tit. 1.13.

28. Cf. F.D. Geley, *Titus* (Interpreter's Bible, 11; New York: Abingdon, 1955), pp. 530-31.

29. The term 'biblical' is meant to include not only the canonical and deutero-canonical books but also the non-canonical works that are closely associated with the scriptural tradition. Often these are pseudepigraphic.

Apostolic Fathers

The Apostolic Fathers reflect a hesitancy (reluctance?) to cite Graeco-Roman traditions; preference is given to 'biblical' sources as authoritative and true. There is, nevertheless, one passage that is striking for its clear dependence on popular mythology to provide a 'prooftext in nature' for the resurrection:

> Let us consider the strange sign which takes place in the East, in the districts near Arabia. There is a bird which is called the phoenix. There is only one of its kind and it lives 500 years and when the time of death's decay draws near, it prepares a virtual tomb of frankincense, myrrh, and other spices. And when the time is completed it enters and dies. Now from the corruption of its flesh there springs a worm, which is nourished by the fluids of the dead bird, and sprouts wings. Then, when it has become strong, it takes up the tomb, in which are the bones of its predecessor, and carries them from the country of Arabia as far as Egypt, until reaching the city of Heliopolis...Do we then consider it great and marvelous that the creator of everything will bring about the resurrection of those who serve in holiness, in the assurance of good faith, when the greatness of his promise is shown even through a bird? (*1 Clem.* 5.1-3; 26.1)

That a respected voice of orthodoxy would accept a myth as an apologetic support was problematic: 'it was considered impossible that a man of Clement's stature could be so mistaken that he would use a fable to gain acceptance for one of the basic tenets of Christian belief'. Thus, some embraced the phoenix myth as true 'since Clement evidently did so'. Many, however, dismissed the epistle as 'spurious' because of its attitude towards the myth.[30] Could it be that attitudes towards the Graeco-Roman poets and philosophers helped shape the issue of Clement's canonicity?[31]

Justin

Within early Christianity, Justin (along with Clement of Alexandria and Origen) is regarded as especially aware of and sympathetic to Graeco-Roman poetry and philosophy. Justin is described as, of all theologians in

---

30. R. van den Brock, *The Myth of the Phoenix* (Leiden: Brill, 1972), p. 4.

31. It seems obvious to ask, why did *1 Clement* fail to be included in the final canonization of the New Testament? The epistle, at one time, had much support for being included with the letters of Paul and the Gospels. Not only is it still found in some ancient manuscripts of the New Testament, but according to Eusebius, *1 Clement* was 'recognized by all' (Eusebius, *Eccl. Hist.* 3.38).

the early church, 'the most optimistic about the harmony of Christianity and Greek philosophy'.[32]

Justin's belief that philosophy not only can be, but *is*, a vehicle of truth is firmly rooted in his personal pursuit of knowledge. This journey led him, ultimately, to Platonism[33] and despite Justin's later conversion to the Christian faith, Plato remained an authority, a source of wisdom, for him. And Socrates, Plato's teacher, was honoured by Justin as a Christ-like philosopher:

> We are taught that Christ is the first-born of God and we have explained that he is the Word within all humanity. Those who have lived by reason were Christians even though they might be called atheists. Such persons among the Greeks were men like Socrates...[34]

It is ironic, however, that Justin's admiration for Socrates is based on an implicit criticism of the Greek poets. Protesting the injustice of the charges against Socrates, Justin comments

> ...what he did was to banish Homer and the other poets,[35] and to instruct people to drive out the evil demons and those who committed those deeds narrated by the poets (*2 Apol.* 10).

At many points Justin seems enthusiastic in his endorsement of 'worldly wisdom' as a glimpse of the divine; yet within his writings is a consistent understanding that the truth of Christianity mocks the impotent theology of Graeco-Roman thought.

The 'venerable old man' who persuaded Justin of the superiority of the gospel founded his claim on a disdain for the achievement of philosophy:

> 'How then,' he said, 'can the philosophers think or say anything true of God, when they have no knowledge of him, having neither seen him at any time, nor heard anyone who has?' (*Dial. Trypho* 3)

The old man insisted that the Hebrew scriptures provided a unique, Spirit-given source of revelation about God[36] and to some degree Justin

---

32. See H. Chadwick, *Early Christian Thought and the Classical Tradition* (Oxford: Oxford University Press, 1966), pp. 5, 9-11.

33. *Dial. Trypho* 2; cf. Philo, *Omn. Prob. Lib.* 13: 'the sacred authority of Plato'.

34. *Apology* 46; cf. Chadwick, *Classical Tradition*, p. 17: 'Justin does not merely make Socrates a Christian. His Christ is a philosopher...'

35. Cf. Plato, *Republic* 377A-379A; 595A-C.

36. *Dial. Trypho* 7.

came to accept that the Graeco-Roman philosophers, even Plato, had often 'borrowed' from this tradition.[37]

This latter objection is common in Hellenistic Judaism and early Christianity and apparently represents a middle position between two extremes. Thus, the 'truth' of philosophy is acknowledged but it is regarded as dependent on the revelation of the scriptures.

This perspective or attitude might be labelled 'the Balaam's ass' view of Graeco-Roman philosophy and poetry. As the donkey provided only an indirect revelation from God (its tongue's 'loosening' was a rare occasion, and its message was made possible only because the donkey had seen the angel of Yahweh) so the philosophy and poetry of the Graeco-Roman world was regarded as, at its best, but an echo of the voice of God in the scriptures.

One Man's Confusing View

The early Church Father, Jerome, exhibits a paradoxical, if not contra-dictory, attitude towards the uneasy association between classical Graeco-Roman literature and the sacred writings embraced by Christianity. On the one hand, in his own spiritual development he came to reject the writings of non-Christians as incompatible with the scripture:

> What agreement is there between Christ and Belial? What has Horace to do with the Psalter, or Virgil with the Gospels, or Cicero with Paul? (Jerome, *Letter* 22.29)

Relating his own story, describing the agony of a deteriorating physical condition, Jerome reports that he was 'caught up in the spirit and brought before the judgement seat' of God. Although he declared him-self to be a Christian, Jerome was harshly rebuked: 'You are lying for you are a Ciceronian, not a Christian'.[38] Devastated, he cried out for mercy and forgiveness. He acknowledged that he would deserve extreme punishment if he should ever again read the works of 'Gentile' (*gentilium*) authors. Jerome then took an oath: 'O Lord if I ever own or read worldly books, I will have denied you' (*Letter* 22.30).

While this experience dramatically illustrates Jerome's (and, to some degree, early Christianity's) contempt for Graeco-Roman literature, he

---

37. *Apology* 44; 59; cf. *Apology* 20.
38. *Letter* 22.30; cf. Augustine, *Confessions* 3.5.

nevertheless frequently quotes from these very writings.[39] One of his correspondents challenged Jerome about the apparent inconsistency:

> At the end of your letter you ask why I sometimes cite examples from secular literature and so defile the purity of the Church with the filth of heathenism (*Letter* 70.2).

Jerome replies that it is appropriate to take the sword from the hand of the enemy, using his own weapon to slay the 'arrogant Goliath'. He further argues that both scripture and the constant proclamation of the church have encouraged a familiarity with the world's 'wisdom'. Jerome maintains,

> It is natural that admiring the beauty of her form and the splendour of her eloquence, I desire to make secular wisdom, my captive handmaid, to be a matron of the true Israel (*Letter* 70.2).

In many respects, the example of Jerome in his ambivalence to Graeco-Roman literature is typical of the attitudes within the early church. There was both a very high regard for Greek philosophy as inspired by God[40] and yet an utter repugnance of the blasphemous mythology and human-centered thought of the Graeco-Roman world.[41] It was believed that in order to be consistent, Graeco-Roman thought either had to be accepted or utterly rejected. Often, like Jerome in his vision, Christianity has regarded Cicero (or Homer or Euripides or Plato) to be in opposition to the scripture, perhaps poisonous to the soul.

The Hellenistic Background of Early Christianity

Because of the church's reluctance to affirm that early Christianity was shaped by the non-biblical world of the Roman Empire, the Graeco-Roman context of the emerging movement has often been dismissed as inconsequential. While the affirmation of the Jewish and Palestinian roots of early Christianity is certainly justified, to emphasize this influence to

39. Jerome often refers to the writings of Virgil and Horace; cf. *Letters* 1.10, 15; 2; 3.3; 6; 7.4; 10.2; 14.3, 4; 16.2; 17.2; 40.2; 49.2, etc.

40. Again see Clement of Alexandria. For example: 'Now O Philosophy, hurry to set before me not only Plato, but many others also, who declare the one and only true God to be God, by his own inspiration...', *Exhortation to the Greeks* 6.

41. This view is found in Tertullian. For example: 'Where is any similarity between Christians and philosophers? Between the disciples of Greece and those of heaven?', *Apology* 46. See especially his *Prescription against Heretics*.

the neglect of significant 'Hellenistic' sources and parallels risks distorting our understanding of Christian origins.[42]

Alexander the Great is perhaps to be regarded as the most important figure in the world of Hellenism.[43] 'Hellenism' may be defined as the Greek culture as it came to permeate the empire of Alexander and in its continuing effect on the Roman world of the early centuries of the Common Era. Before his premature death, as Alexander had conquered territory, his policies intentionally promoted Hellenistic principles. In particular, his establishing of Greek cities as 'administrative centres' and a spirit of tolerance towards foreign customs and beliefs served to nurture Hellenism in the East.[44]

The death of Alexander could have led to the political and cultural fragmentation of his kingdom as there had been minimal time for Hellenistic influences to permeate a united empire. Yet the most significant force which provided continuing unity to the post-Alexander Hellenistic world was the common language *koine*.[45]

Greek became widespread throughout the area of Alexander's conquests, including Palestine. The evidence for the prevalent use of Greek in first-century Palestine is overwhelming.[46] Consequently, the language

---

42. Cf. S.J. Case, *The Evolution of Early Christianity* (Chicago: University of Chicago Press, 1942), pp. 30-31; R. Scroggs, 'The Earliest Hellenistic Christianity', in J. Neusner (ed.), *Religions in Antiquity* (Leiden: Brill, 1968), p. 176. Cf. R.M. Grant, 'Hellenistic Elements in 1 Corinthians', in A. Wikgren (ed.), *Early Christian Origins* (Chicago: Quadrangle Books, 1961), p. 65: 'The Church had roots in Judaism, though sometimes modern scholars are tempted to exaggerate the depth of the roots; it came to its flowering in the Greco-Roman world. Perhaps we could say, borrowing Paul's metaphor, that Palestine planted, Hellas watered, but God gave the growth.'

43. Cf. the statement of D.S. Russell, *The Jews from Alexander to Herod* (Oxford: Oxford University Press, 1967), p. 7: 'Alexander set himself the task of bringing together into one the civilizations of east and west, on the basis of that Greek culture which he himself had inherited and of which he was an avowed champion.'

44. J.E. Stambaugh and D.L. Balch, *The New Testament in its Social Environment* (Philadelphia: Westminster, 1986) pp. 13-14; V. Tcherikover, *Hellenistic Civilization and the Jews* (Philadelphia: The Jewish Publication Society of America, 1959), p. 91. Cf. Russell, *Jews*, pp. 7-8, 23-24.

45. M. Hengel, *Judaism and Hellenism* (Philadelphia: Fortress Press, 1974), p. 58. Cf. E. Stagg and F. Stagg, *Woman in the World of Jesus* (Philadelphia: Westminster, 1978), p. 55.

46. Hengel, *Judaism*, pp. 56-57, 60-61, 104; Tcherikover, *Hellenistic Civilization*, p. 265; S. Lieberman, *Hellenism in Jewish Palestine* (New York: The Jewish

itself of early Christian literature must be regarded as at least implicit evidence that Hellenism influenced the primitive church:

> It remains one of the most momentous linguistic convergences in the entire history of the human mind and spirit that the New Testament happens to have been written in Greek—not in the Hebrew of Moses and the prophets, nor in the Aramaic of Jesus and his disciples, nor yet in the Latin of the imperium Romanum, but in the Greek of Socrates and Plato, or at any rate in a reasonably accurate facsimile thereof, disguised and even disfigured though this was in the koine by the intervening centuries of Hellenistic usage.[47]

At the outset, then, it must be acknowledged, simply with regard to language, that 'the debt of Christianity to the Graeco-Roman world is undeniable'.[48] And it is virtually inevitable that this language would have carried the ideas, implications, concepts, and imagery of the Hellenistic era.[49]

Consequently, important insights are being made into the relationship between early Christian traditions and significant parallels in Graeco-Roman literature. Recognizing the possibility, even the likelihood, of influence is prompting the consideration of exciting questions. This is certainly true of Pauline and Lukan studies[50] and has opened up areas of research in the teaching of Jesus.

Theological Seminary of America, 1962); E. Bickerman, *From Ezra to the Last of the Maccabees* (New York: Schocken Books, 1962); B.L. Woolf, *The Background and Beginnings of the Gospel Story* (London: Ivor Nicholson & Watson, 1935), pp. 65-66; M. Smith, 'Palestinian Judaism in the First Century', in M. Davis (ed.), *Israel: Its Role in Civilization* (New York: Arno, 1956), pp. 67-81; Jaeger, *Early Christianity*, p. 6; Case, *Evolution*, p. 29.

47. J. Pelikan, *Christianity and Classical Culture* (New Haven, CT: Yale University Press, 1993), p. 3; F.C. Grant, *Roman Hellenism and the New Testament* (Edinburgh: Oliver & Boyd, 1962), p. 21. Cf. W.R. Schoedel and R.L. Wilken (eds.), *Early Christian Literature and the Classical Intellectual Tradition* (Paris: Editions Beauchesnes, 1979), p. 9; G.E. Ladd, *The Pattern of New Testament Truth* (Grand Rapids, MI: Eerdmans, 1968), p. 11.

48. Grant, *Roman Hellenism*, p. 20.

49. W. Jaeger, 'Paideia Christi', *ZNW* 50 (1959), p. 2. Cf. Grant, *Roman Hellenism*, p. 21.

50. Many sources might be cited. Reference will only be given, at this point, to A. Deissmann, *Light from the Ancient East* (New York: George H. Doran, 1927), pp. 300-301 and two more recent studies: Malherbe, *Paul and the Popular Philosophers*; and N.A. Dahl, *Jesus in the Memory of the Early Church* (Minneapolis, MN: Augsburg, 1976), pp. 87-98.

As the culture of first century Galilee comes more to light, it appears increasingly probable that Jesus spoke some Greek. The pervasiveness of ὑποκριτής in the Synoptic tradition and its virtual absence from the LXX imply a firsthand knowledge by Jesus of the dramatic actor, who assumed a role and identity that were not truly his own and performed for the audience's approval.[51]

While it is very reasonable to be cautioned to avoid the dangers of 'parallelomania',[52] for a well-balanced and accurate description of Christian origins attention must be given to the Graeco-Roman context of early Christian literature.[53] Such is the intention of these essays: to offer an understanding of how certain themes, stories, and concepts from the Hellenistic world *may well have* influenced the teachings and writings of the early Christians.

While the explicit use of so-called classical texts is indeed rare in the New Testament,[54] there are numerous similarities that warrant attention. Some can only be mentioned, others will be explored more fully in the essays that follow.

Some Intriguing Parallels

Sacrifice
In an apocryphal (i.e., non-biblical) tradition Jesus explained the purpose of his ministry in these words:

---

51. R.A. Batey, 'Jesus and the Theatre', *NTS* 30 (1984), p. 563.

52. S. Sandmel, 'Parallelomania', *JBL* 81 (1962), p. 1: 'We might for our purposes define parallelomania as that extravagance among scholars which first overdoes the supposed similarity in passages and then proceeds to describe source and derivation as if implying literary connection flowing in an inevitable or predetermined direction.' See also R. Renehan, 'Classical Greek Quotations in the New Testament', in D. Neiman and M. Schatkin (eds.), *The Heritage of the Early Church* (Rome: Pontificium Institutum Studiorum Orientalium, 1973), p. 21; E.F. Scott, 'The Limitations of the Historical Method', in S.J. Case (ed.), *Studies in Early Christianity* (New York: Century, 1928), pp. 3-18.

53. Cf. Case, *Evolution*, pp. v, vi. See the general observation in L.G. Patterson, *God and History in Early Christian Thought* (New York: Seabury, 1967), p. 16: 'The life of the age which Christians believed had entered upon its last days was dominated by the classical or Greco-Roman civilization.'

54. Renehan, 'Greek Quotations', p. 45; cf. H.R. Minn, 'Classical Reminiscence in St Paul', *Prudentia* 6 (1974), pp. 93-98.

> I am come to do away with sacrifices, and if you do not cease from
> sacrificing, the wrath of God will not cease from you.[55]

This statement is far more explicit than any found in the canonical
Gospels, which portray Jesus as holding a 'prophetic' view of sacrifice.[56]
While it may seem unreliable as a word of the historical Jesus, this logion
has striking parallels within Graeco-Roman literature despite the fact that
animal sacrifice was virtually universal in the first century CE.[57]

Nearly seventy years ago a study was published drawing attention to
the remarkable similarities between Pythagoras and Jesus.[58] One view
they may have shared was that the gods or God only wanted bloodless
sacrifices. Apollonius of Tyana claimed to follow strictly the example of
Pythagoras in refusing to participate in rites of animal sacrifice.[59] This
repugnance of 'blood-stained altars' characterizes the attitude of certain
philosophers and of a later emperor. Seneca writes

> the honour that is paid to the gods lies, not in the victims for sacrifice,
> though they be fat and glitter with gold, but in the upright and holy desire
> of the worshippers. Good men, therefore, are pleasing to the gods with an
> offering of meal and gruel; the bad, on the other hand, do not escape
> impiety although they dye the altars with streams of blood.[60]

Expressing a similar perspective, the emperor Julian (reigned 361–363
CE) argued

> ...all offerings whether great or small that are brought to the gods with
> piety have equal value, whereas without piety, I will not say hecatombs,
> but, by the gods, even the Olympian sacrifice of a thousand oxen is merely
> empty expenditure and nothing else.[61]

---

55. Epiphanius, *Panarion* 30.16.4-5, referring either to the Gospel of the
Hebrews or the Gospel of the Ebionites.

56. F.M. Young, *Sacrifice and the Death of Christ* (London: SPCK, 1975), p. 47.

57. Young, *Sacrifice*, p. 21. Mention should also be made of the parallels with
the Essenes; cf. Philo, *Omn. Prob. Lib.* 75.

58. I. Lévy, *La Légende de Pythagore de Grèce en Palestine* (Paris: Bibliotheque
de L'Ecole des Hautes Etudes, 1927).

59. Philostratus, *Life of Apollonius of Tyana* 1.1-2; 4.16; 8.7; cf. P. Gorman,
Pythagoras (London: Routledge & Kegan Paul, 1979), p. 75.

60. Seneca, *On Benefits* 1.6.3.

61. Julian, *To the Cynic Heracleios* or *Oration* 7.213D.

Self-mutilation

The synoptic Gospels indicate that Jesus taught that out of self-interest alone, one ought to be willing to sacrifice a part of the body in order to gain a greater good:

> If your right eye causes you to stumble, pluck it out and throw it away. It is better that you lose one of your members than that your whole body be thrown into Gehenna (Mt. 5.29).

> If your hand causes you to stumble, cut it off. It is better for you to enter life maimed than to have two hands and to go to Gehenna, the unquenchable fire…And if your foot causes you to stumble, cut it off. It is better to enter life lame than to have two feet and to be thrown into Gehenna…And if your eye causes you to stumble, tear it out. It is better for you to enter the kingdom of God with one eye than to have two eyes and be thrown into Gehenna (Mk 9.43, 45, 47).

While this teaching lacks a significant background in the Hebrew scripture, a remarkable parallel is found in Plato's *Symposium*:

> People are willing to have their hands and feet cut off if they are persuaded that those members are bad for them (Plato, *Symposium* 205E).

Is this merely gruesome hyperbole or might these passages indicate that a form of self-mutilation was practised in the Graeco-Roman world?

Self-giving Love

Plato's *Symposium* also provides several significant parallels to the Johannine tradition. While not directly relevant, it is striking in this connection that the Platonic Socrates, in contrast to that of Xenophon, is regarded as a Johannine-like portrait of the man:

> Only love will make a person willing to sacrifice one's own life for another (Plato, *Symposium* 179B).

> No one has greater love than this, to lay down one's life for one's friends (Jn 15.13).

Again the Graeco-Roman tradition provides a striking environment for early Christian thought.

Using Judges outside the Community

Paul's admonition of the Corinthians seems to echo a passage from the *Republic*. Both the apostle and the philosopher criticize the failure of a community to ensure justice through its members:

Do you not think that it is disgraceful, even an indication of being ill-bred, to make use of judges imported from others—who then become your masters—because of your own inabilities? (Plato, *Republic* 405A, B)

When any of you has a grievance against another, do you dare to take it to court before the unrighteous, instead of taking it before the saints? Do you not know that the saints will judge the world? And if the world is to be judged by you, are you incompetent to try trivial cases? Do you not know that we are to judge angels—to say nothing of ordinary matters? If you have ordinary cases, then, do you appoint as judges those who have no standing in the church? I say this to your shame. Can it be that there is no one among you wise enough to decide between one believer and another, but a believer goes to court against a believer—and before unbelievers at that? (1 Cor. 6.1-6)

Surely the context of early Christianity must include the literary and cultural world of the Graeco-Roman era. As Jerome was certainly aware of many similarities to the writings of the Christians in the Greek and Roman poets and philosophers, it is the intention of these essays first to call attention to the social and even linguistic setting of early Christian literature and, secondly, to explore the apparent significance of specific 'parallels'. Several terms, ideas, and themes will be the subject of investigation. No particular thesis is being defended; it is enough to have the reader consider possibilities.

Chapter 2

APHRODITE AND 1 CORINTHIANS

Introduction

While I was a boy, when I read in Homer and Hesiod about wars and quarrels, not only of the demigods but of the gods themselves, and besides about their amours and assaults and abductions and lawsuits and banishing fathers and marrying sisters, I thought that all these things were right, and I felt an uncommon impulsion toward them.

But when I came of age, I found that the laws contradicted the poets and forbade adultery, quarreling, and theft. So I was plunged into great uncertainty, not knowing how to deal with my own case. For the gods would never have committed adultery and quarreled with each other, I thought, unless they deemed these actions right, and the lawgivers would not recommend the opposite course unless they supposed it to be advantageous. Since I was in a dilemma, I resolved to go to the men whom they call philosophers...begging them to deal with me as they would, and to show me a plain, solid path in life.[1]

Paul refers to his own 'maturing': 'When I was a child, I spoke like a child, I thought like a child, I reasoned like a child; when I became an adult, I put an end to childish ways' (1 Cor. 13.11). Again we ask, more specifically, whether Paul recognized a need to mature in faith and character and whether he was suggesting that his readers 'grow up'.

In this chapter on love, Paul was perhaps calling the Corinthians to the high demands of ἡ ἀγάπη and directing his readers to abandon their notions about the gods and those concerning Aphrodite, the so-called

---

1. Lucian, *Menippus* 3 (trans. A.M. Harmon). Cf. Seneca, *Epistulae Morales* 4.2; Xenophanes quoted in Sextus Empiricus, *Against the Mathematicians* 1.289; 9.193; see also Euripides, *Bellerophon* fragment 292; Clement of Alexandria, *Exhortation to the Greeks* 4; Plato, *Republic* 378B; Origen, *Against Celsus* 1.17; Philostratus, *Life of Apollonius of Tyana* 5.14. Cf. Daniélou, *Gospel Message*, p. 16; J.A. Scott, *Homer and his Influence* (New York: Cooper Square, 1963), p. 76.

goddess of love, and Eros[2] in particular.[3] This possibility raises the question of Paul's attitude towards Aphrodite reflected in 1 Corinthians.

Within the Graeco-Roman world in which early Christianity emerged, the goddess Aphrodite (Venus or the Cyprian goddess[4]) won widespread devotion and allegiance because she was regarded as the power, indeed the source, of life-giving love. She was considered the one who controlled the irrationality of passion and the pleasures of sex. Aphrodite, significantly, was even hailed as the ruler of Rome.[5]

Lucretius's praise of the goddess's omnipotence in the natural world is dramatic.[6] Through her ability to inspire sexual desire and her association with Eros, Aphrodite had near dominance in the supernatural realm as well. While Artemis, Athene, and Hestia could resist the goddess's power, Zeus, the mightiest of the gods, was considered Aphrodite's slave.[7]

Zeus, however, exerted power over Aphrodite that she might have sexual desire for a mortal, Anchises. This effectively took away the goddess's boast that she alone could cause the immortals to mate with humans.[8] Aphrodite and Anchises were drawn by desire to each other but the goddess used cunning and deception, even to the point of denying her divinity,[9] in order to persuade the herdsman to have sex with her.

---

2.   Eros was regarded in some traditions as the son of Aphrodite: Plato, *Phaedrus* 242D; Cicero, *Nature of the Gods* 3.23.

3.   Cf. Case, *Evolution*, p. 177: 'it was not easy to persuade the Corinthians to sever their former connections with idolatry or to abandon the heathen vices in which "some" of them had been steeped.'

4.   M.C. Howatson (ed.), *The Oxford Companion to Classical Literature* (Oxford: Oxford University Press, 1989), p. 592. For the association of Aphrodite with Cyprus see E. Hamilton, *Mythology* (Boston: Little, Brown, 1942), p. 33. See also E.J. Goodspeed, *Paul* (Philadelphia: Winston, 1947), pp. 39, 40; D. Soren and J. Jones, *Kourion* (New York: Doubleday, 1988), p. 58.

5.   Ovid, *Amores* 1.8.42.

6.   He writes '...for you alone govern the things of nature since without you nothing comes into existence...' *De Rerum Natura* 1.1-22; D. Kinsley, *The Goddesses' Mirror* (Albany, NY: SUNY Press, 1989), p.193.

7.   *Homeric Hymn V* 1-39; cf. Euripides, *Hippolytus* 4; *Trojan Women* 948-50; Plutarch, *Eroticus* 752, 756, 770; Kinsley, *Mirror*, pp. 188-89; A.L.T. Bergen, 'The Homeric Hymn to Aphrodite: Tradition and Rhetoric, Praise and Blame', *Classical Antiquity* 8 (1989), pp. 5-6: 'Aphrodite reigns supreme'.

8.   *Homeric Hymn V* 45-55, 247-55.

9.   *Homeric Hymn V* 109-10.

Twice Anchises is described as seized by ἔρος,[10] and, significantly, *the gods willed their coming together*.[11] Consequently Aphrodite's actions in Greek mythology were often regarded as examples of divinely approved yet seductive and deceptive behaviour that came to characterize the sexual conduct within the society and culture of the Graeco-Roman world.

Strabo (first century CE) observed that Aphrodite was worshipped throughout the early Empire and that numerous temples were established in her honour.[12] Presumably the rites associated with the cult(s) of Aphrodite lasted several centuries; Eusebius (third and fourth centuries CE) praised Constantine for abolishing some of these practices. Referring to an isolated shrine 'dedicated to the filthy demon Venus', Eusebius condemned the unlawful immorality which typified the activity of those who met for worship. Constantine, learning of their behaviour, 'commanded that the building and the offering be completely destroyed'.[13]

Several writers in early Christianity harshly rebuke the mythology and immorality associated with the goddess. Lactantius claimed that Aphrodite was responsible for the 'prostitute's art'[14] and Clement of Alexandria regarded her as 'a deified harlot'.[15] With Antisthenes, Clement desired to injure Aphrodite.[16] Theophilus described her as 'shameless'.[17] This stern judgment[18] was likely based on the Christians' awareness that Corinth was famous in the Graeco-Roman world for its temple of Aphrodite which may well have featured cultic prostitutes.[19] Consequently, it is

---

10. *Homeric Hymn V* 91, 144.

11. *Homeric Hymn V* 166. Thus this 'adulterous' union was sanctioned by the gods! The child of their union was Aeneas (*Homeric Hymn V* 196-98).

12. Strabo 8.3.12; Kinsley, *Mirror*, p. 185; R.M. Grant, *Gods and the One God* (Philadelphia: Westminster, 1986), p. 23.

13. Eusebius, *Life of Constantine* 3.55; cf. 3.58 and *Oration* 8.5-6; see also, G. Grigson, *The Goddess of Love* (New York: Stein & Day, 1977), p. 140.

14. Lactantius, *Divine Institutes* 1.17.

15. Clement of Alexandria, *Exhortation to the Greeks* 2.12.

16. *Strom.* 2.20. For the 'wounding' of Aphrodite see *Iliad* 5.336-51.

17. Theophilus, *Ad Autolycum* 3.3.

18. Jerome even longs to see Venus on Judgment Day! *Letter* 14.11.

19. Strabo 8.6.20; Pausanias, *Description of Greece* 2.1.1-5.2; Pindar, fragment 122. B. MacLachlan, 'Sacred Prostitution and Aphrodite', *SR* 21/22 (1992), pp. 145-62; Kinsley, *Mirror*, p. 207; Grigson, *Goddess*, p. 111; Goodspeed, *Paul*, pp. 90-91. But compare J. Murphy-O'Connor, *St Paul's Corinth* (Wilmington, DE: Glazier, 1983), pp. 127-28.

expected that Paul would have regarded Aphrodite as a disgusting symbol of the deity and that he might express this as a warning to the Corinthians especially as Corinth was considered by its culture to be a city 'favoured by Aphrodite'.[20]

My concern in this essay is with the unanticipated silence of Paul regarding Aphrodite even as he wrote to the Corinthians addressing the issues of prostitution and sexual immorality; and I hope to show how this affected his attitude towards sex as expressed in the letter. Early Christianity had no reluctance to utter the name of the goddess and Paul himself acknowledged in 1 Corinthians that 'there are many so-called gods' (8.5); yet the apostle chose to be silent when an indictment of Aphrodite is anticipated. His decision must be regarded as significant.[21]

The Aphrodite Mythology

In the surviving ancient Greek literary tradition there are two principal views regarding the 'birth' of Aphrodite. In Homer she is one of Zeus's many offspring, daughter of Dione.[22] For Hesiod, by contrast, Aphrodite emerged from the foam of the ocean that surrounded the castrated genitals of Ouranos, the 'grandfather' of Zeus.[23] This significant discrepancy allowed for the later interpretation that there were actually two

---

20. Cf. A.D. Nock, *St Paul* (New York: Harper & Row, 1963), p. 241; Goodspeed, *Paul*, pp. 90-91; Dio Chrysostom, *Orations* 37.34; cf. Grant, *Gods*, p. 24. The Corinthian celebration of Aphrodite and the cultic practice of prostitution likely was related to an ancient Babylonian tradition that is reported by Herodotus (1.199):

> The foulest Babylonian custom is that which compels every woman of the land once in her life to sit in the temple of Aphrodite and have intercourse with some stranger... After the intercourse she has made herself holy in the goddess's sight and goes away to her home... There is a custom like to this in some parts of Cyprus.

21. Cf. Grant, *Gods*, pp. 22-24 where Luke's choice not to mention Aphrodite is called 'significant'.

22. *Iliad* 3.374; 5.131, 312, 348, 370-71, 820; 20.105; *Odyssey* 8.308; see also *Homeric Hymn III* 195; *Homeric Hymn V*, 81, 107, 191; Sappho, *Hymn to Aphrodite* (cf. the reference by Dionysius of Halicarnassus quoting Sappho, *On Literary Composition* 23). For a recent statement of the difference between Homer's and Hesiod's views see Grigson, *Goddess*, p. 33.

23. *Theogony* 180-91. Cf. M.R. Dexter, *Whence the Goddesses* (New York: Pergamon, 1990), pp. 112-13.

goddesses: an earthly (or common) and a heavenly Aphrodite.[24]

Many assumed that the name 'Aphrodite' is derived from the term ἀφρός which means 'foam'. Homer, however, would not have been likely to accept this view because the 'foam' theme is not part of his understanding of Aphrodite's origin. Sappho may have held another etymological explanation. The irrationality of sexual passion is regarded as central to the power of Aphrodite[25] and interestingly, the word ἀφροσύνη means 'crazed'.[26] Perhaps the name of Aphrodite is closely associated with this madness.[27]

One of the earliest stories about Aphrodite is found in the traditions that lie behind the *Iliad*. A challenge is set before the immortals to decide which goddess is the most beautiful. Zeus chooses not to make such a decision himself, so a human, a shepherd named Paris, is selected to be the judge. Athene and Hera seek to win his approval but Aphrodite successfully bribes Paris with promises that he will enjoy the love of the most beautiful woman on earth, Helen (who is Zeus's daughter).[28]

Ultimately the goddess is held responsible for the Trojan War[29] for with Aphrodite's help Paris takes Helen away from Greece to his home in Troy.[30] During the long battle between Greece and the Trojans. Aphrodite rescues Paris from death[31] and in saving her son Aeneas she is actually wounded.[32] The goddess assists Hera in seducing (and deceiving) her husband Zeus.[33] Near the end of the struggle as the

24. See below, pp.38-9. Cf. Plotinus, *Ennead* 3.5 where Aphrodite is described as 'double'; cf. Plato, *Symposium* 180D.

25. W.F. Wyatt, 'Sappho and Aphrodite', *Classical Philology* 69 (1975), pp. 213-14. See also Euripides, *Bacchae* 402-405.

26. See *Iliad* 7.110. In Plato, *Protagoras* 332E folly is regarded as the opposite of σωφροσύνη. See also in the Cynic Epistles attributed to Diogenes 49.

27. Cf. Euripides, *Trojan Women* 989-90: 'The foolishness of men is their Aphrodite; sensual/senseless—how similar!' Cf. Virgil, *Georgics* 3.266-67; *Homeric Hymn V* 253-54; Philostratus, *Life of Apollonius of Tyana* 1.33.

28. Euripides, *Trojan Women* 398: 'Paris wedded Zeus' child.'

29. Hamilton, *Mythology*, pp. 256-59. Cf. Euripides, *Trojan Women* 948: 'Punish that goddess!'

30. Cf. *Iliad* 3.38-65 where Hector taunts Paris about the gifts of Aphrodite; *Odyssey* 4.261; *The Cypria*.

31. *Iliad* 3.369-83. And after rescuing Paris she brings him and Helen together to make love, 3.383-448. Cf. Clement of Alexandria's comment in *Exhortation to the Greeks* 2.30.

32. *Iliad* 5.311-51.

33. *Iliad* 14.193-221.

various deities are supporting either the Greeks or the Trojans, Pallas
Athene physically attacks Aphrodite (who is helping the injured Ares).[34]

In the *Odyssey* a tale is sung of Aphrodite's unfaithfulness to her
husband-god, Hephaestus. Her adultery with Ares is mocked as she and
her lover are trapped by Hephaestus's net and the other gods come in
to witness their humiliation. Despite the apparent shame of Ares'
predicament, Apollo expresses a willingness, even an eagerness, to take
his place beside the goddess.[35] This story seemed to regard unfaithfulness as humorous and lust or sexual desire as, in some sense, 'godly'.

While many of the earlier myths feature the beauty, sexuality and
vanity of the goddess, Aphrodite's vindictive character is well illustrated
in the myths of Myrrha[36] and Hippolytus.[37] In both of these stories
Aphrodite 'confers lust or desire on mortals' in order to destroy those
who offend her dignity.[38] She says of Hippolytus:

> Of all his contemporaries only this man dares to say I am a despicable
> deity... I will punish him today for I resent his affront.[39]

Hippolytus, in his steadfast rejection of the enticement of sex, is portrayed as truly god-like. 'While Aphrodite sinks to the level of a mortal
and below, Hippolytus, though mortal, rises to the level of the divine.'[40]
He is the appropriate companion of Artemis, the virgin goddess.

Lust (ἐπιθυμία) was regarded as a weapon which Aphrodite used to
maintain and exercise dominion over both the gods and human beings.
For Plato, as long as the individual remains subject to the passions of
sexuality it is as though that person were a slave. Sophocles' words
indicating that old age sets a person free from servitude to Aphrodite are

---

34. *Iliad* 21.415-33.

35. *Odyssey* 8.266-367.

36. Apollodorus 3.9.1; 3.14.3; Ovid, *Metamorphoses* 10.298-518; Hyginus,
Fabulae 58.242; Pindar, *Pythian Odes* 2.15-17. Myrrha's child was Adonis, the
object of Aphrodite's affection.

37. Euripides, *Hippolytus*. Cf. the reference to Aphrodite in Plutarch, *Septem
Sapientium Convivium* 146D.

38. C.G. Brown, 'The Power of Aphrodite: *Bacchylides* 17,10', *Mnemosyne* 44
(1991) p. 335.

39. Euripides, *Hippolytus* 22-24, 37-39. Cf. D. Kovacs, 'Euripides *Hippolytus*
100 and the Meaning of the Prologue', *Classical Philology* 75 (1980), p. 133.

40. Kovacs, '*Hippolytus*', p. 135.

endorsed: 'Gladly have I escaped...as though I had run away from an angry and brutish master.'[41]

Sophocles regarded Aphrodite (and Eros) as wielding iresistible power. In *Antigone*, following the dramatic confrontation between Creon and Haemon where the latter's love for Antigone will lead to his doom, the chorus chants:

> Love ("Ερως) is unconquered in battle...not even the immortals can escape...
> Invincible Aphrodite works her purpose.[42]

Sophocles' contempt for Aphrodite (and Eros) is reflected in his charge that desire for a woman led to the death of Heracles.[43]

In Greek mythology Aphrodite, through her control and manipulation of the sexual urge in gods and mortals, appears as a powerful goddess. Few can resist her influence and Aphrodite is portrayed as vain and vengeful, intent on exercising dominion. She is recognized as the tragic force responsible for the humiliation of gods and the death of humans.[44]

Despite this apparent hostility towards Aphrodite, Eros, especially in the thought attributed to Socrates, came to be highly regarded both as a god and as a virtue. Even the erotic poetry of Sappho is described as a manifestation of the 'Socratic art of love' intended for disciples.[45]

---

41. Plato, *Republic* 329B-D; Philostratus, *Life of Apollonius of Tyana* 1.13; cf. Philo, *Spec. Leg.* 3.69; Plutarch, *Love of Wealth* 524A. However, see also Plutarch, *Quaestiones Convivales* 654C,D.

42. *Antigone* 781-800. This is echoed in *Trachiniae* 497-517. See also Sophocles, fragment 941 where Aphrodite is described as 'death...raving madness...continual longing...Who is not subject to this goddess?', in A.C. Pearson, *The Fragments of Sophocles* (Cambridge: Cambridge University Press, 1917), III, pp. 106-10. Cf. also Plutarch, *Eroticus* 770.

43. *Trachiniae* 354-55, 488-89, 860-61. Cf. R. Scodel, *Sophocles* (Boston: Harvard University Press, 1984), p. 29: 'This is the work of Aphrodite', and p. 38: 'The tragedy is the work of Aphrodite and her associate Eros, the deities of sexual passion.'

44. Cf. Patricia Marquardt's observation that in Hesiod, Aphrodite 'even when she seems an obvious good' nevertheless retains 'a destructive potential': 'Hesiod's Ambiguous View of Women', *Classical Philology* 77 (1982) p. 283. Apparently as a response to the title of the previous article Eva Canterella comments, 'Hesiod's vision of women contains no ambiguity': *Pandora's Daughters* (Baltimore, MD: Johns Hopkins University Press, 1987), p. xix. Cf. also Stagg and Stagg, *Woman in the World of Jesus*, pp. 56-57.

45. Maximus of Tyre, *Orations* 18.9.

The eros of the spirit was given greater value than the eros of the body:[46]

> Deep as the sensual roots of Platonic love may be, its whole tendency is
> to seek deliverance from the merely sensual. Plato does all in his power to
> prevent the confusion or identification of the Eros which he has in mind,
> with ordinary sensual love.[47]

This perspective implies that there were actually *two* Aphrodites: (1) the
heavenly, who inspires a type of 'spiritual' love; and (2) the earthly, who
is responsible for the physical, sexual impulses of eros. Thus Homer and
Hesiod's differing accounts of the goddess's origin find resolution.[48]

The Christian Use of ἀγάπη
The New Testament distinguishes between the love characteristic of the
gospel and the passion that promotes sexual immorality:

> Be imitators of God as beloved (ἀγαπητὰ) children. And walk in love (ἐν
> ἀγάπη) as Christ loved (ἠγάπησεν) us and gave himself up for us, a
> fragrant offering and sacrifice to God. But fornication (πορνεία) and all
> impurity or covetousness must not even be named among you, as is
> fitting among saints (Eph. 5.1-3).

It is quite apparent that early Christianity regarded use of the term ἔρως
as being inappropriate to designate either God's love for humanity or for
the Christian's responsibility to show love to others.[49] The term ἔρως is
not found in the New Testament literature, presumably because of its
association with immorality, and it is found only once in the Apostolic
Fathers.[50]

These statistics are suggestive. If early Christianity associated ἔρως
with ἐπιθυμία and πορνεία,[51] then this provides some explanation for
the apparent substitution of ἀγάπη for ἔρως. Thus, the condemnations
of Aphrodite found in several writers in the early church would be, in all

46. Xenophon, *Symposium* 8.12; Plato, *Symposium* 181B.
47. A. Nygren, *Agape and Eros* (trans. P. Watson; Philadelphia: Westminster,
1953), pp. 50-51. Cf. Plato, *Symposium* 181E-182A which criticizes the πανδήμους
ἐραστὰς as often guilty of unlawful and immoral conduct. Attention could be drawn
to a number of references in *Phaedo*, but mention ought to be made of the use of
ἀφροδισίων in 64D.
48. Xenophon, *Symposium* 8.9-10; Plato, *Symposium* 180D-E; 181A-C; cf.
Herodotus 1.105, 131; Pausanias 22.3; Lucian, *Dialogues of the Courtesans* 295. It
is of interest to note that Philo does not believe that Plato is serious (*Vit. Cont.* 59)!
49. Nygren, *Agape*, p. 33.
50. Ignatius, *Rom.* 7.2.
51. Cf. *Did.* 3.3: ὁδηγει ἡ ἐπιθυμία προς τὴν πορνείαν.

probability, suggestive of Paul's own attitude.

This would in turn offer various insights into the background of some important features of 1 Corinthians where a reference to Aphrodite is to be expected. In the absence of explicit mention of the goddess it is important to consider the apostle's intentions.

The so-called hymn to love in 1 Corinthians 13[52] is seen to be a deliberate exaltation of ἀγάπη over ἔρως. Despite the seeming 'parallels' in Graeco-Roman literature[53] which would make ἔρως understandable, even anticipated, Paul selects the 'less common word' ἀγάπη filling it with the emerging (or revealed) Christian view of love.[54] Paul avoids any reference to sexual attraction, or even 'romantic' love in ch. 13.

There are several indications in 1 Corinthians that the apostle is confronting the social and moral effects of the mythology associated with Aphrodite. Further, Paul's specific awareness of the rituals associated with the Aphrodite cult in Corinth would have influenced the manner in which he addressed certain issues. Both Paul's general attitude toward Graeco-Roman mythology and his apparent familiarity with the stories involving Aphrodite shaped this letter.[55]

One particular feature of 1 Corinthians warrants our attention in this essay: the problem of immorality—both individually in one case and among the men of the community in another.

The Effects of the Aphrodite Traditions on Paul's Letter

Aphrodite's association with sexuality, seduction, and adultery certainly implicated her as a dangerous influence on the Christians throughout the Empire.

---

52. See also 1 *Clem.* 49.

53. H. Conzelmann, *1 Corinthians* (Philadelphia: Fortress Press, 1975), pp. 219-20.

54. C.T. Craig, *1 Corinthians* (Interpreter's Bible, 10; New York: Abingdon, 1953), p. 166; cf. p.167: '*Agape* is not to be confused with sensual attraction for the opposite sex.' Cf. the comment by Wayne Meeks on a separate topic: 'A new vocabulary appeared in talk about what one ought to do and why' (*The Origins of Christian Morality* [New Haven, CT: Yale University Press, 1993], p. 2). For an important argument for balance in this discussion see G. Quispel, 'God is Eros', in W.R. Schoedel and R.L. Wilken (eds.), *Early Christian Literature and the Classical Intellectual Tradition* (Paris: Editions Beauchesnes, 1979), pp. 189-205.

55. But it must be acknowledged that the letters of Paul themselves show 'only the slightest acquaintance with pagan Greek literature': Nock, *St Paul*, p. 236.

> Every lust (ἐπιθυμία) is at war against the spirit and the immoral (πόρνοι)...will not inherit the kingdom of God.[56]

This warning of Polycarp is not unique; it is a typical expression which emerges from early Christianity's repudiation of immorality and its concern for the 'entrance requirements' for the eschatological community.[57] This emphasis is to be found throughout the letters of Paul:

> For the lusts of the flesh (σάρξ ἐπιθυμεῖ) are against the spirit... Now the works of the flesh are obvious: immorality (πορνεία)... I warn you, as I warned you before, that those who commit such deeds will not inherit the kingdom of God (Gal. 5.17, 19, 21).

> Do you not know that the unrighteous will not inherit the kingdom of God? Do not be deceived—the immoral (πόρνοι)...will not inherit the kingdom of God (1 Cor. 6.9-10; cf. Eph. 5.5).

Paul was concerned that Christians should live by 'kingdom standards' that set a code of strict morality, a righteousness perhaps even more rigorous than that of the Pharisees (cf. Mt. 5.20). The apostle was outraged by the specific πορνεία found within the Corinthian Christian community. Paul's own Pharisaic background prompted him to write that Christians are

> not to associate with anyone who bears the name of brother (or sister) if that person is immoral (πόρνος)...not even to eat with such a person.[58]

The Pharisaic repudiation of immorality was rooted in the Hebrew scripture. Yet Paul was also aware of the secular culture's standards of morality. The Corinthians permitted, even boasted of, a scandalous

---

56. Polycarp, *Phil.* 5.3.

57. Cf. 1 Pet. 2.11; Jas 4.1-3. See R. Garrison, *Redemptive Almsgiving in Early Christianity* (JSNTSup, 77; Sheffield: JSOT Press, 1993), pp. 9-11.

58. 1 Cor. 5.11; cf. Mk 2.15-16. Perhaps Paul regarded immorality as making a person 'impure': L.W. Countryman, *Dirt, Greed and Sex* (Philadelphia: Fortress Press, 1988), p. 105. Cf. also Countryman's observation that during the New Testament period, 'the Pharisees seem to have concentrated their attention on issues of table fellowship', p. 53. Cf. also S.S. Bartchy, 'Table Fellowship with Jesus and the "Lord's Meal" at Corinth', in R.J. Owens, Jr and B.E. Hamm (eds.), *Increase in Learning* (Manhattan, KS: Manhattan Christian College, 1979), p. 55; J.D.G. Dunn, 'Jesus, Table-Fellowship, and Qumran', in J.H. Charlesworth (ed.), *Jesus and the Dead Sea Scrolls* (New York: Doubleday, 1992), p. 260.

situation that was not even accepted among non-Jewish peoples (ἔθνεσιν, 1 Cor. 5.1-2).[59]

It would seem, then, that Paul had a general perception of non-Jewish morality: (1) that it permitted lust and passion within marriage (cf. 1 Thess. 4.4-5), and (2) that it had some scruples about sexual behaviour that the Corinthian Christians had violated.[60]

Paul, in painfully confronting this Corinthian immorality, chose to challenge but not to identify his 'enemy'. The prevailing influence of the Aphrodite cultic practices in the city had promoted a freedom that expressed itself in immorality. Paul sought to rescue his readers from the potential for destructiveness; he writes, 'Cleanse out the old leaven that you may be a new lump, as you really are unleavened' (5.7).

The Corinthian immorality was not restricted to one or two individuals. Paul is indignant that certain male members of the community are known to have been involved with prostitutes[61] and they apparently felt that their 'freedom in Christ' allowed this. The apostle, while conceding that 'all things are lawful to me', nevertheless insists that participation in the body of Christ excludes the possibility that one would be united with a prostitute (6.12-15). The idea, repugnant to the apostle, is repudiated by his 'most emphatic negation μὴ γένοιτο'.[62]

Although some have attempted to identify these prostitutes with the priestesses of Aphrodite,[63] it is more prudent, certainly more defensible, simply to claim that Paul was conscious that

> the prostitute in Corinth, as well as in many other ancient cities, was dedicated to the service of pagan gods. To resort to such a person was to effect union with the god she served.[64]

---

59. Cf. K. Quast, *Reading the Corinthian Correspondence* (New York: Paulist, 1994), p. 44.

60. See P. Brown, *The Body and Society* (New York: Columbia University Press, 1988), p. 51: Paul 'looked out with undisguised disgust at the tedious prospect of the sins of the gentile world. In that dark landscape, sexual sins cluttered the foreground.'

61. Brown, *Body*, p. 51.

62. This is the only occurrence of the phrase in 1 Corinthians; Craig, *1 Corinthians*, p.74. Cf. Meeks, *Origins*, p. 94, who translates the phrase 'unthinkable'. For the significance of the phrase in Paul see A.J. Malherbe, '*Me Genoito* in the Diatribe and Paul', *HTR* 73 (1980), pp. 231-40.

63. Cf. Craig, *1 Corinthians*, p. 74.

64. W.F. Orr and J.A. Walther, *1 Corinthians* (AB; Garden City, NY: Doubleday, 1976), p. 203.

The Graeco-Roman culture regarded Aphrodite as the enticing power behind all sexual behaviour, not only that within marriage[65] but also that considered to be immoral. Indeed, Aphrodite's adultery among the gods and with mortals gave divine precedence (and permission) to much of the sexual conduct within Graeco-Roman society. Paul wished to challenge the dominion of the goddess in announcing that by the indwelling of the Spirit, followers of Christ were to show that they were free from slavery to lust and ought to 'glorify God in their bodies' (6.12-20).

It is not surprising to find that Paul repudiates πάθει ἐπιθυμίας as characteristic of the non-Jewish peoples in their ignorance of God. He apparently condemns lust even within marriage where the spouse is the object of desire,[66] and he insists that Christian marriage be honourable and holy (1 Thess. 4.3-7).[67] It is unexpected, however, when he nevertheless argues that passion and an absence of self-control are in fact the primary basis for getting married (1 Cor. 7.1-9, cf. v. 36).[68] It is natural to conclude from the chapter that Paul would maintain that lust is in fact appropriate within marriage. Yet the apostle is unwilling to endorse ἐπιθυμία in his instructions to the Corinthians. Sexual desire and a lack of self-control are permitted but 'lust' is not explicitly sanctioned. While the term is certainly anticipated and even implied, it is in fact absent.

The apostle's general attitude towards women is already implicit in his advice to the Corinthians in 7.1—'it is good for a man not to touch a

65. Cf. Musonius Rufus, 'Is Marriage a Handicap for the Pursuit of Philosophy?', lines 20-30. C.E. Lutz, 'Musonius Rufus "The Roman Socrates"', *Yale Classical Studies* 10 (1947), p. 95

66. The translation and interpretation of σκεῦος are controversial. Nevertheless, Paul is clearly confronting the issues of sexuality and marriage. See F.F. Bruce, *1 and 2 Thessalonians* (Waco, TX: Word, 1982), pp. 80-88; O.L. Yarbrough, *Not Like the Gentiles* (Atlanta: Scholars Press, 1985).

67. Cf. Philo, *Spec. Leg.* 3.8-10; Pseudo-Phocylides 193-94.

68. Among many commentators see Quast, *Corinthian Correspondence*, p. 51; E.S. Fiorenza, *In Memory of Her* (New York: Crossroad, 1989), p. 223: 'those who are tempted should have intercourse with their own wives or husbands'; Orr and Walther (*1 Corinthians*, p. 211) write that Paul 'affirms that remarriage is preferable to the consuming *passion* that they may experience if they are unable to exercise such *self-control* as makes possible his own estate'; M.Y. MacDonald, 'Women Holy in Body and Spirit', *NTS* 36 (1990), p. 163; M.E. Thrall, *The First and Second Letters of Paul to the Corinthians* (Cambridge: Cambridge University Press, 1965), p. 52; R.S. Kraemer, *Her Share of the Blessings* (Oxford: Oxford University Press, 1992), pp. 138-39; For marriage as a means to avoid immorality, see Yarbrough, *Not Like the Gentiles*, pp. 89, 96.

woman' (καλὸν ἀνθρώπῳ γυναικὸς μὴ ἄπτεσθαι).[69] This sentiment is reinforced a few verses later when Paul tells the unmarried and the widows that it is good (καλὸν) that they remain single as he has (7.8; cf. v. 26). Avoiding the temptation to have sexual contact with women is regarded as a sign of virtue.

In exalting the decision to avoid, to reject, the sexual relationship inherent in marriage Paul has left the clear implication that the man who unites with a woman, even with his wife, is somehow deficient in self-control (cf. 7.5, 9). In so doing the man seems to have chosen what is less than good, or at the least the one who refrains from marriage does better (7.38).[70]

Paul regarded marriage and women in particular as potentially dangerous vehicles of temptation that might be exploited by Satan (cf. 7.5).[71] In counselling the Corinthians to avoid sexual relationships and to enter into them only within the context of marriage, Paul sought to overcome the dangerous and prevailing influence of the cults of Aphrodite.

Conclusion

Undoubtedly, the mythology of both the Greeks and Romans had a profound effect upon the ancient world, influencing beliefs, standards, and behaviour. Specifically, the character and actions of the goddess Aphrodite shaped the Graeco-Roman attitudes toward sexuality in general and to the particular morals associated with sexual conduct. The widespread influence of the cults of Aphrodite, as they infiltrated society, would certainly have only reinforced those values.

During the early centuries of the Roman Empire the temple of Aphrodite and its prostitutes/priestesses made Corinth a prominent (and, from the Christian perspective, glaring) example of the goddess's influence on religion as well as culture. As Corinthian citizens accepted the Christian message, many believed that their 'freedom in Christ' allowed them to continue their sexual practices.

In writing his first (extant) letter to the Corinthian Christians, Paul had to respond to the immorality that characterized the church. He also confronted the prevailing attitudes of his readers towards love and sexual

---

69. Cf. *T. Reub.* 6.1: 'Protect your senses from women.'

70. Paul stresses that the unmarried individual will have greater opportunity to serve the Lord. Cf. Philo, *Hypothetica* 11.17.

71. For a striking parallel to 1 Cor. 7.5 see *T. Naph.* 8.8.

intercourse and he did so with the intention of promoting a Spirit-filled perspective. Consequently, the apostle challenged the Corinthians with regard to their former belief in the gods. He is silent, however, concerning Aphrodite (at least by name).

In all probability Paul was contemptuous of the mythology of the non-Jewish peoples and regarded it as virtually blasphemous even to give recognition to the gods and goddesses of their tradition. Or perhaps, in his own way, Paul was ironically endorsing the goddess's own words: 'know that I am not a goddess. Why do you compare me to the immortals?'[72]

---

72. *Homeric Hymn*, V, pp. 109-10.

Chapter 3

FRIEND OF TAX COLLECTORS

Introduction

The Gospel tradition reports that Jesus was considered 'a glutton and a drunkard' (Mt. 11.19//Lk. 7.34). This indictment, which certainly seems to be related to the charge in Deut. 21.18-21,[1] apparently arose out of disgust with the association of Jesus and his disciples with certain types of people who were regarded as disreputable: 'Why do you eat and drink with tax collectors and sinners?' (Lk. 5.30). Jesus' participation in table fellowship with those who were rejected was criticized because it was understood to be an act of friendship and therefore an implicit acceptance of their style of life.

The common table was an 'ideal' in both distinctly Hellenistic as well as Jewish traditions[2] and often served to promote the virtue of hospitality;[3] indeed the theme of hospitality is prominent in early Christian literature.[4] Certain features of the background of the Graeco-Roman world with regard to the symposium and the significance of sharing meals offer a fascinating context for understanding Jesus as a friend of tax collectors and sinners.[5]

1. J. Jeremias, *The Parables of Jesus* (New York: Charles Scribner's Sons, 2nd rev. edn, 1972), p. 160. Cf., however, J.A. Fitzmyer, *The Gospel according to Luke I–IX* (Garden City, NY: Doubleday, 1981), p. 681.

2. Dunn, 'Jesus, Table-Fellowship, and Qumran', p. 255 refers to Ovid, *Metamorphosis* 8.613-70 and Genesis 18.

3. Cf. *Odyssey* Book 7.

4. Garrison, *Redemptive Almsgiving*, pp. 81-82.

5. See J.H. Neyrey, 'Ceremonies in Luke–Acts: The Case of Meals and Table Fellowship', in J.H. Neyrey (ed.) *The Social World of Luke–Acts* (Peabody, MA: Hendrickson, 1991), pp. 361-387.

The Symposium in the Graeco-Roman World
Within Hellenistic society, the meal at dinner was normally followed by
'the second course of the traditional banquet'[6] which was the so-called
symposium or drinking party. The symposium was regarded as an
opportunity to discuss ideas, to share philosophical insights, and to enrich
friendships.[7] Plutarch maintained that this practice was observed even by
those who were not part of the aristocracy:

> ...after the meal even ordinary and uneducated people permit their thoughts
> to wander to those other pleasures which are far-removed from the
> concerns of the body.[8]

The dinner party and thus the symposium represented one of the few
forms of entertainment within private homes for the Greeks and Romans.[9]
The symposium has properly been described as 'an immensely popular
and ubiquitous social custom in classical antiquity'.[10]

The Symposium as a Literary Genre
Inasmuch as the symposium was a central feature of the lives of people
in the Hellenistic era and served an 'important function in their scheme
of social intercourse', it is only to be expected that the imagery, themes,
and setting of the dinner party would make significant contributions to
the literature of that period. In this regard Aune maintains that Plutarch's
Septem Sapientium Convivium is a clear example of a distinctive genre,
one which used the dinner party as the 'framework' for a narrative or
discourse.[11]

Perhaps the two most influential examples of this genre in ancient

6.   D.E. Smith, 'Table Fellowship as a Literary Motif in the Gospel of Luke',
JBL 106 (1987), p. 614.

7.   Cf. G. Paul, 'Symposia and Deipna in Plutarch's *Lives* and in Other
Historical Writings', in W.J. Slater (ed.), *Dining in a Classical Context* (Ann Arbor:
University of Michigan, 1991), p. 157. Cf. also D.E. Smith, 'Social Obligation in the
Context of Communal Meals' (ThD Dissertation, Harvard Divinity School, 1980),
p. 2.

8.   Plutarch, *Quaestiones Convivales* 673A; Smith, 'Social Obligation', p. 38.

9.   L.R. Shero, 'The *Cena* in Roman Satire', *CP* 18 (1923), p. 126.

10.   D.E. Aune, '*Septem Sapientium Convivium* (*Moralia* 146B-164D)', in
H.D. Betz (ed.), *Plutarch's Ethical Writings and Early Christian Literature* (Leiden:
Brill, 1978), pp. 70-71. Cf. W. Burkert, 'Oriental Symposia: Contrasts and Parallels',
in Slater (ed.), *Dining in a Classical Context*, p. 7. Cf. B. Mack, *A Myth of Innocence*
(Philadelphia: Fortress Press, 1988), p. 81.

11.   Aune, '*Septem Sapientium Convivium*', p. 53; cf. p. 58.

literature were the *Symposia* of Plato and Xenophon, both providing an account of Socrates at a meal as the honoured guest.[12] Indeed, according to Philo, these were the two most significant banquets held in Greece.[13]

While the symposium genre was widespread and influential from the fifth century BCE until the fourth century CE,[14] it was nevertheless of apparently restricted, virtually minimal, significance in shaping primitive Christian literature. The earliest example of a Christian symposium was composed by Methodius about 300 CE.[15] Although the literary genre itself may not have had a great effect on early Christian literature, the symposium as a social convention certainly had an impact on the Christian practices associated with sacred meals.[16]

The Symposium and the New Testament

The New Testament clearly provides evidence that the δεῖπνον was used as a 'literary vehicle' for several of the sayings of Jesus.[17] Perhaps the most dramatic example is found in John 13–16.[18] Yet all other New Testament instances of a dinner as the setting for teaching are restricted to the Lukan writings. Luke was 'the most literary' of the Gospel writers and as an author he deliberately adapted certain literary conventions with which he was familiar.[19] Particular attention has been given to the symposium theme in Luke's Gospel[20] and has focused on the significant

12. Smith, 'Table Fellowship', p. 615.

13. Philo, *Vit. Cont.* 57.

14. See J. Martin, *Symposion: Die Geschichte einer literarischen Form* (Paderborn: Schoningh, 1931); E.S. Steele, 'Luke 11.37-54—A Modified Hellenistic Symposium?', *JBL* 103 (1984), p. 393.

15. Aune, '*Septem Sapientium Convivium*', pp. 69-70.

16. Aune, '*Septem Sapientium Convivium*', pp. 60, 75.

17. Aune, '*Septem Sapientium Convivium*', pp. 69-70. Cf. K.E. Corley, 'Were the Women around Jesus really Prostitutes? Women in the Context of Greco-Roman Meals' (SBL Seminar Papers; ed. D. Lull; Atlanta: Scholars Press, 1989), p. 487.

18. The term δεῖπνου occurs in 13.2, 4 but 14.31b is problematic for the view that chs. 15 and 16 are part of the 'table talk'.

19. Fitzmyer, *Luke I–IX*, p. 5; Smith, 'Table Fellowship', p. 613. Cf. W.S. Kurz, SJ, 'Luke 22.14-38 and Greco-Roman and Biblical Farewell Addresses', *JBL* 104 (1985), pp. 252, 253, 257.

20. Two recent studies are Steele, 'Luke 11.37-54—A Modified Hellenistic Symposium?' and Smith, 'Table Fellowship'. Cf. also X. de Meeus, 'Composition de Lc. XIV et Genre Symposiaque', *ETL* 37 (1961), pp. 847-70; H. Moxnes, 'The Social Context of Luke's Community', *Int* 48 (1994), pp. 383-84.

features of table fellowship as an anticipation of the messianic banquet in the kingdom of God.[21] The meal setting in Luke provides the context for several theological ideas to be discussed or highlighted in the Gospel.

One prominent motif in his writings is that God chooses those whom society has rejected. This is clearly emphasized in Luke's understanding of the cross as a distinct perversion of justice[22] and the subsequent resurrection as a reversal of the human verdict on Jesus.[23] It is evident, however, even in the early chapters of his Gospel that Luke gives special attention to the theme that God chooses to exalt those who are humbled, whether or not their subjection is actually voluntary.[24]

Luke employs the meal imagery to indicate that anticipated standards have been overturned and that there will be unexpected guests at the messianic banquet:

> Someone asked Jesus, 'Master, will only a few be saved?' He said to them, 'Earnestly try to enter through the narrow door, for I tell you many will try to enter but not be able. When the owner of the house has gotten up and shut the door, and you standing outside knock at the door saying "Lord open to us", he will reply, "I do not know where you come from". Then you will say, "But we ate and drank with you and you taught in our streets". But he will reply, "I do not know where you come from. Go away from me you evildoers!"
>
> There will be weeping and gnashing of teeth when you see Abraham, Isaac, and Jacob and all the prophets in the kingdom of God while you are thrown out. And people will come from east, west, north, and south to eat in the kingdom of God. Indeed, some who are last will be first, and some who are first will be last' (Lk. 13.23-30).

This expectation is reinforced in the teaching of Jesus regarding those who should be invited to feasts. Ironically, these instructions are part of

---

21. Dunn, 'Jesus, Table-Fellowship, and Qumran', p. 256.

22. Acts 8.33; See especially Lk. 23.4, 14-15, 22; Marshall remarks, 'The innocence of Jesus could not be more firmly underlined': *Commentary on Luke* (Grand Rapids, MI: Eerdmans, 1978), p. 861.

23. Acts 2.22-24; 3.13-15.

24. Cf. Elizabeth (1.25); Mary (1.48), in Mary's song of praise, 'he has exalted those who are lowly' (1.52); the appearance of the angels to shepherds, on which Fitzmyer comments 'News of the birth of the Messiah is first made known, not to religious or secular rulers of the land, but to lowly inhabitants of the area... The chord of "the lowly" has already been struck in Mary's Magnificat (1.52) and foreshadows the use of it in the Gospel proper (see the "Q" passage in 7.22)' (*Luke I–IX*, p. 408).

the 'table talk' when Jesus himself was at a meal with some Pharisees (14.1, 7, 15):

> He said to the one who had invited him, 'When you have a banquet or dinner, do not invite your friends, your brothers, your relatives, or your rich neighbours, lest they in return invite you, and you would be repaid. Instead, when you have a banquet, invite the poor, the maimed, the lame, and the blind. Because they cannot repay you, you will be blessed, repaid at the resurrection of the righteous' (Lk. 14.12-14).

While these instructions are clearly opposed to Hellenistic principles of reciprocity in gift-giving, even as an 'open antithesis to the conventions of antiquity',[25] still there is a remarkable parallel found in Plato:

> ...if you ought to grant favours to those who ask for them most eagerly, you ought to do good not to the best but to the needy for they will be extremely grateful for the relief. At private banquets you ought not to invite your friends, but beggars and those in need of a meal. For these will love (ἀγαπήσουσιν) you and follow you to your doors, being delighted and grateful, calling down blessings on your head.[26]

This significant passage in the Graeco-Roman tradition might suggest that Luke himself is to be regarded as the creator of the emphasis found in the teachings of Jesus, using Jesus to promote certain values he himself holds. Undeniably, Luke has used the stories regarding Jesus' eating and drinking with tax collectors and sinners to illustrate the theme that 'salvation has come to the "poor", a term that is given symbolic reference to the idea of social outcasts in general'.[27] While this is certainly feasible, it is, nevertheless, plausible that the historical Jesus was in fact denounced as a glutton and a drunkard, a friend of disreputable people.

Jesus and Table Fellowship

It is unnecessary to suspect that here the influence of Graeco-Roman practices, particularly the customs of the symposium and table fellowship as a context for teaching, only became significant as Luke composed and structured his Gospel. Kathleen Corley's cautious observation warrants serious consideration; she writes that 'it is...not impossible to imagine that Jesus and his followers, *like other Hellenistic peoples*, found the

25. G. Stahlin, 'φιλέω', *TDNT* 9 (1974), p. 160.
26. Plato, *Phaedrus* 233D-E. But cf. Stahlin, 'φιλέω', p. 160, n. 117.
27. Smith, 'Table Fellowship', p. 636. Cf. Bartchy, 'Table Fellowship with Jesus', p. 55.

meal setting to be a natural place for discourse to occur'.[28]

If it was known and remembered that the teaching of Jesus often 'began as "table talk"', then two Markan comments—both of which are deleted by Matthew and by Luke—may have a special significance:[29]

> ...and the crowd again came together so that they could not even eat (Mk 3.20).

> For so many were coming and going they had no leisure to eat (Mk 6.31).

These seemingly irrelevant observations may be rooted in an awareness that the meal setting provided many opportunities for Jesus to teach. In fact it is reasonable to believe that Jesus engaged in 'table talk' as a means of discourse and that this was one of his methods for teaching those around him.[30]

Among those in his company were tax collectors and sinners. That this is a plausible, historically reliable proposition is too often taken for granted. Yet the fact that Mt. 11.19//Lk. 7.34 seems to have its origins in a 'taunt' from his opponents suggests that the description is likely to have come from 'the time of Jesus' ministry'.[31]

In order for this indictment of Jesus to be historically relevant to his own *Sitz im Leben*, it is enough to show that some of the Pharisees would have been outraged by his association with tax collectors and sinners.[32] Surely, in light of such explicit passages as Sir. 9.16,[33] one

28. Corley, 'Women around Jesus', p. 488 (italics mine).

29. Dunn, 'Jesus, Table-Fellowship, and Qumran', p. 255.

30. This is almost certainly related to the intriguing fact that several traditions of the resurrection reflect an interest in the themes of eating and drinking: Lk. 24.13-35, 36-42; Jn 21.4-14; Acts 10.40-41. The use of συναλιζόμενος in Acts 1.4 may refer to Jesus 'taking salt' (eating) with the disciples. A striking 'proverb' that bears on this is found in Cicero, *On Friendship* 19. Cf. also Plutarch, *Table-Talk* 697D: 'the most truly divine seasoning at the table is the presence of a friend...not because of his eating and drinking with us, but because he joins in the sharing of conversation.'

31. J. Jeremias, *New Testament Theology* (London: SCM, 1975), p. 115. Cf. M. Hengel, *The Charismatic Leader and his Followers* (New York: Crossroad, 1981), p. 55: 'with Jesus one cannot detect any trace of the basic rabbinical injunction, always to seek fellowship and discussion with other scholars or individuals of like mind'.

32. Dunn, 'Jesus, Table-Fellowship, and Qumran', p. 260. Cf. Hengel, *Charismatic Leader*, p. 60; B. Chilton, *A Feast of Meanings* (Leiden: Brill, 1994), pp. 31, 66; J. Neusner, *From Politics to Piety* (Englewood Cliffs, NJ: Prentice Hall, 1973), p. 73.

33. 'Let the righteous be your dinner companions.'

may rightly conclude that 'it was basic to the Pharisees' understanding of God's Law that the pious could have table fellowship *only* with the righteous'.[34] The historical reliability of the accusation that Jesus ate and drank with social outcasts is the best explanation of its appearance in the Gospel tradition. After Easter, the scandal of the gospel, the focal point of criticism, was the crucifixion of Jesus.[35]

34. Bartchy, 'Table Fellowship', p. 54; Dunn, 'Jesus, Table-Fellowship, and Qumran', p. 260. See A. Hull, *Jesus in Bad Company* (New York: Avon, 1972), pp. 32-34.

35. Jeremias, *New Testament Theology*, p. 121.

Chapter 4

LAST WORDS

Introduction

Whether as a dramatist or a historian reporting the life and achievements
of individuals, a writer often emphasizes the final, dying words of a
subject.[1] What is remembered can greatly affect how that person is
regarded. Tacitus, in his description of the death of Galba, recognizes
that his sources of information offer differing testimony as to whether
the emperor died as a genuine statesman[2] or as a desperate man seeking
to bribe his would-be assassins:[3] 'His last words are variously recorded
by the conflicting voices of hatred and admiration'.[4] Unconcerned with
the historical reliability of the accounts available to him, Tacitus says of
Galba's death, 'Little did the murderers care what he said'.[5] Plutarch,
however, apparently prompted by his interest in the political virtue of his
subject,[6] chooses to report the more 'noble' version of the last words.

Richard A. Batey raises some important questions in asking, 'How
does the development of the Gospels as genre compare to the dramatic
literature of the Hellenistic Roman stage? How does Jesus himself compare to the tragic hero?'[7] I hope to begin to address these issues. I will

---

1. Cf. R.E. Brown, *The Death of the Messiah* (New York: Doubleday, 1994),
p. 1045.

2. Cf. Plutarch, *Galba* 27, which claims that Galba's last words were addressed
to his approaching assassins, 'Complete your task if it is better for the Roman people'.

3. Cf. Suetonius, *Galba* 20.

4. Tacitus, *Histories* 1.41 (trans. K. Wellesley).

5. *Histories* 1.41.

6. Cf. C.P. Jones, *Plutarch and Rome* (Oxford: Clarendon Press, 1971),
pp. 73-74.

7. Batey, 'Jesus and the Theatre', p. 572. I also acknowledge the influence of
F.G. Downing's '*A Bas les Aristos*: The Relevance of Higher Literature for the
Understanding of the Earliest Christian Writings', *NovT* 30 (1988), pp. 212-30.

argue that Luke, the historian and theologian, was similarly aware of differing reports of the last words of the character that dominates his narrative.[8] Deliberately rejecting Mark's account and presenting another version,[9] Luke, like Plutarch, sought to promote certain themes and impressions that he wished to give to his readers. The principal concern in this essay is the nature of that impression.

It is necessary first, however, to give attention to the issue of what material was available to Luke as he shaped his narrative.

Luke's Sources

Luke indicates his awareness of other 'compiled' information about Jesus and his teaching.[10] The clear meaning of 1.1-4 is that the author has evaluated and reworked this material in his own effort to produce an accurate and orderly account.

The prevailing two-source theory need not be defended here; it is assumed to be a comprehensive and reliable view of the literary relationships between the synoptic Gospels. According to this hypothesis, Luke used the Gospel of Mark[11] (and the sayings source Q) as he constructed his own record of Jesus. Our concern, then, is to gain a provisional understanding of Mark's intention in reporting the last words of Jesus. This is particularly critical because Luke chooses to reject or modify his Markan source with regard to this significant feature of the passion narrative.

8. Cf. the observation by J.E. Powell: 'The last words of Jesus on the cross are variously reported': 'Father, into Thy Hands', *JTS* 40 (1989), p. 95. See also P.W. Walaskay, 'The Trial and Death of Jesus in the Gospel of Luke', *JBL* 94 (1975), pp. 81-93.

9. I reject the idea that Luke had a special 'passion source' available to him that he preferred to Mark. While Vincent Taylor (*The Passion Narrative of St Luke* [ed. O.E. Evans; Cambridge: Cambridge University Press, 1972]) and Joachim Jeremias ('Perikopen-Umstellungen bei Lukas', *NTS* 4 [1958], pp. 115-119) favour this theory, I have found the arguments of Frank Matera ('The Death of Jesus according to Luke: A Question of Sources', *CBQ* 47 [1985], pp. 469-85) and M.L. Soards (*The Passion according to Luke* [JSNTSup, 14; Sheffield: JSOT Press, 1987]) more persuasive. Cf. Brown's analysis, *Death*, pp. 67-75.

10. J.C. O'Neill has written a very provocative essay touching on this: 'The Lost Written Records of Jesus' Words and Deeds behind our Records', *JTS* 42 (1991), pp. 483-504.

11. Cf. Brown, *Death*, pp. 42-46.

Mark's Last Words of Jesus

In Mark the final words of Jesus in the entire Gospel[12] are 'My God, my God, why have you forsaken me?' (15.34; cf. Ps. 22.1). This cry haunts the reader; does Jesus die rejected by God? And inasmuch as Mark reports no Easter appearance of the risen Lord, the dying words of Jesus raise christological questions that concern the understanding of his present status.

Matthew, while also recording the so-called cry of dereliction (27.46), overcomes its potential theological difficulties by the triumphant claim of the risen Jesus, 'All authority in heaven and earth has been given to me [by God the Father]' (28.18; cf. 11.27). Mark, however, so constructs his narrative that the anguished words of the dying Jesus echo even as the Gospel closes. Why?

While Mark's Gospel begins with an indication that the coming of 'good news' commences in the person of Jesus (1.1), as the story unfolds the reader senses imminent tragedy;[13] the 'good news' comes to be associated with a sense of shame or rejection, going so far as to be connected with the idea of crucifixion (8.34-38). This permits, even encourages, the question whether Mark, to some degree, modelled his presentation on the story of a tragic hero. Did Mark regard Jesus as similar to a specific literary character?

Several figures from Greek mythology offer themselves as potentially significant models for Mark's Jesus. Prometheus is one example of a suffering hero, 'crucified' by Zeus:[14]

---

12. It is probable that 16.8 is the original conclusion of Mark. See A.T. Robertson, *Studies in Mark's Gospel* (ed. H.F. Peacock; Nashville: Broadman Press, 1958), p. 128: 'What we must say in the light of textual criticism is that none of the various additions to verse 8 can possibly be a part of the original Gospel.'

13. Cf. G.N. Stanton's remarks: 'Many features of Mark's gospel would have puzzled readers familiar with the techniques of ancient biographical writing...To readers...the gospels would recall either some of the elements of a biography, or of a theological treatise, or perhaps even of a tragedy': *The Gospels and Jesus* (Oxford: Oxford University Press, 1989), pp. 19-20. See also T.J. Weeden, *Mark—Traditions in Conflict* (Philadelphia: Fortress Press, 1971), pp. 11-18. Surely the claim of David Rhoads and Donald Michie is extreme: 'No earlier literary document bears the *slightest* resemblance to Mark's' (italics mine): *Mark as Story* (Philadelphia: Fortress Press, 1982), p. xii.

14. See M. Hengel, *Crucifixion* (Philadelphia: Fortress Press, 1977), pp. 11-12. Cf. Lucian, *Zeus Catechized* 8.

Oh that he had hurled me below the earth…so that no god or other kind would now gloat over this my agony! But, as it is, I am a plaything of the winds; to my misery, I suffer ills whereat my foes exult.[15]
I will drain to the dregs my present lot until such time as the mind of Zeus shall abate its wrath.[16]

Hermes responds to the cries of Prometheus by commenting, 'Wherein does his prayer fall short of raving?'[17] Many have made a similar judgment of Jesus' cry in Mk 15.34.

On the other hand, while the parallels with the Markan portrait of Jesus from Gethsemane to his death are intriguing, the character of Prometheus seems an unlikely model for two principal reasons: (1) he is not a son of God;[18] and (2) he does not die.[19] The Markan Jesus has certain Promethean features,[20] but in Mark's Christology it is essential to recognize the identity of Jesus as God's son and it is central that he died; in these respects Jesus is clearly different from Prometheus.

If in fact Mark modelled his story of Jesus on the tragedy of a mythological figure, it is significant to recognize that Heracles offers a remarkable parallel. He was reputed to be the *begotten* son of Zeus[21] (by a human mother). Heracles performed many mighty deeds before suffering an agonizing death.[22] It is perhaps coincidental, but nevertheless

15. Aeschylus, *Prometheus Bound* 152-59 (trans. H. Weir Smyth). Cf. Mk 15.29-32.

16. *Prometheus Bound* 377-78. Cf. Mk 14.36.

17. *Prometheus Bound* 1056-57.

18. Given the response of the centurion (Mk 15.39), it must be central to Mark that Jesus, even in dying, be recognized as God's son (cf. 1.1, 11; 3.11; 5.7 etc.). The use of ἀληθῶς in the centurion's evaluation indicates a decisive judgment on his part. That Luke revises his source to have the centurion declare the *innocence* of Jesus suggests that Luke intends to emphasize different themes in reporting the death of his subject. Cf. Marshall, *Luke*, p. 874.

19. Cf. the boast, 'Why should I fear whose fate is not to die?', Aeschylus, *Prometheus Bound* 934. Indeed, Prometheus is confident that eventually he will be released from his torture. Cf. lines 168-79; 189-95.

20. Mention ought to be made of Prometheus's gifts to humanity, even sparing mortals from the wrath of Zeus. Aeschylus, *Prometheus Bound* 106-10; 236-38; 250-54. Cf. Lucian, *On Sacrifices* 6.

21. Cf. Sophocles, *The Women of Trachis* 1106, 1185; Euripides, *Alcestis* 1136-37; Apollodorus 2.4.7-8.

22. Sophocles, *The Women of Trachis*. See R. Graves, *The Greek Myths* (Harmondsworth: Penguin, 1990), II, pp. 200-202.

of interest, that Sophocles regarded the *last words* of Heracles to be a potential source of revelation.[23]

Mark's apparent reluctance to speak of Jesus as the *begotten* son of God or even to mention his birth suggests that although he may have been influenced by the story of Heracles, Mark chose to avoid comparisons of the two heroes.[24] There are, nevertheless, noteworthy similarities.

Mark immediately identifies his subject as God's son (1.1),[25] one more powerful (ὁ ἰσχυρότερός) than John the Baptist, God's messenger (1.2, 7). The deeds of Jesus are described as 'mighty works' (cf. 6.2) and he is regarded as the virtual embodiment of power (5.30; cf. 6.14). By his presence alone he is able to subdue the demon-possessed man whose strength was unparalleled (5.1-6) and the crazed man anticipates torture from this 'Mighty One': 'What have you to do with me, Jesus, *Son of the Most High God*? I adjure you by God, do not torment me' (5.7; cf. 1.24). Indeed, Jesus' power over the demons is regarded as evidence that he has overcome the 'strong man', even Satan (3.23-27).[26] While significant differences must be recognized between the two accounts, it is reasonable to conclude that a powerful son of God in the literature of Mark's cultural environment provided a model by which he understood (and portrayed) Jesus.

The inevitability of Heracles' death is foreshadowed. At one point he is blinded by a spirit of insanity that provokes him to murder his wife and children. Crushed by guilt, grief, and despair, Heracles considers the option of suicide. In this context the chorus expresses a sympathy that eerily anticipates the anguish of Mark's readers as they find Jesus crying out in pain, 'My God, my God, why have you forsaken me?' Watching in horror the chorus calls

> Ah Zeus, why this stern hate against thy son? Why hast thou brought him to this sea of ills?[27]

---

23. *The Women of Trachis* 1149-50.

24. Could John's use of μονογενῆ have had a similar purpose? The only begotten son of God is Jesus; there are no others.

25. The textual reading υἱοῦ θεοῦ is supported by B, D, W *et al.*

26. Among the mighty deeds attributed to Heracles are his conquering Death (*Alcestis* especially lines 97-98, 105), and his invasion of Tartarus to capture Cerberus (his so-called Twelfth Labour). An interesting parallel to the Markan passage is found in the comparison of the gods of love and war in Plato, *Symposium* 196d.

27. Euripides, *The Madness of Heracles* 1086-87 (trans. A.S. Way).

Because of the compassion and friendship of Theseus, Heracles chooses not to end his own life despite his agony and self-hate. Still, however, it is fated that one day he will die. Much later when Heracles prepares to offer a sacrifice, he drapes himself with a cloak, unaware that it has been soaked with the venomous blood of a centaur he has slain. The poison torments Heracles and he is unable to relieve its effects; he is racked with pain, dying slowly. He cries out to his father

O Zeus! Torture, torture is all you give me![28]

Heracles ends his agony by having others, including his son,[29] burn his body on a pyre. The story of Heracles then claims that his spirit is received among the gods after his death. Zeus embraces him as his noble son and Heracles is welcomed in Olympia.[30]

Again there are important differences between Mark's Jesus and the mythological Heracles,[31] but there are remarkable parallels between these two 'mighty' sons of God who suffer agonizing deaths and question the purpose of their father. The possible influence of the literary tradition about Heracles on Mark may provide insight into his intentions in reporting the last words of Jesus to be, 'My God, my God, why have you forsaken me?'

The literary world of Mark's readers included a son of God whose father permitted him to suffer a miserable death. Heracles had protested Zeus's sanction of his torture and yet through his dying Heracles came into a greater glory than he had known in his mortal condition.

Within this literary (and theological!) context in the Graeco-Roman culture of his day, perhaps Mark used the last words of Jesus to draw harsh attention to the agony of his execution and to confront his readers with God's apparent approval of the death of his son. Jesus' divine sonship would be recognized through his death as the centurion's statement clearly proves: 'Truly this man was God's son!' (15.39).[32]

---

28. Sophocles, *The Women of Trachis* 996-97 (trans. M. Jameson).

29. In an ironic parallel (?) with Lk. 23.46, Heracles cries out, 'My son, my son! Where are you? Help me here, lift me up!' (*The Women of Trachis* 1024-25) where the dying one entrusts himself into the hands of his *son*.

30. Ovid, *Metamorphoses* 9.241-73.

31. Among these is the feature of physical strength itself and the fact that Heracles is portrayed as a man of violence.

32. Matera, 'The Death of Jesus', p. 480.

Luke's Last Words of Jesus

In adapting the Markan report, which was one of his principal sources of information about the suffering and death of Jesus, Luke edited, revised, and supplemented this material. In so doing Luke worked as a historian, a theologian, and, for our purposes, most significantly as an author.[33]

To understand Luke's intentions, the interpreter must be alert to the author's 'obvious concern to relate his account of the Christ-event...to a Greco-Roman literary tradition'.[34] Such is our task as we consider Luke's use of Mark.

While Luke's passion narrative disagrees with the Markan report in several respects, four features of the Lukan divergence are of particular interest here:

1. The omission of the cry, 'my God, my God, why have you forsaken me?'
2. The inclusion of the saying, 'Father into your hands I commit my spirit' (23.46; cf. LXX Ps. 30.6).
3. The juxtaposition of the final words of Jesus and the centurion's reaction (23.46-47).
4. The alteration of the centurion's statement to 'Certainly this man was just' (δίκαιος; 23.47).[35]

The last detail is especially revealing and enables us to interpret Luke's purpose and intention in changing Mark.[36] The theme of Jesus' *innocence* is central in the Lukan passion narrative.[37] Initially, then, we might suspect that Luke's choice in his reporting of the last words of Jesus was influenced by his overwhelming interest in the just character of his subject.

33. 'Recent Lucan studies have emphasized more and more that Luke was the first consciously Christian literary writer': Fitzmyer, *Luke I–IX*, p. 5.

34. Fitzmyer, *Luke I–IX*, p. 58. Cf. Smith, 'Table Fellowship', p. 613. See also V.K. Robbins, 'Prefaces in Greco-Roman Biography and Luke–Acts', *PerRS* 6 (1979), p. 94.

35. For rendering this term as 'just', cf. R.J. Karris, 'Luke 23.47 and the Lucan View of Jesus' Death', *JBL* 105 (1986), pp. 65-74. Cf. Matera, 'The Death of Jesus', p. 479.

36. Powell comments, 'All these difficulties have disappeared in Luke' ('Father, into Thy Hands', p. 95).

37. Stanton, *Gospels*, p. 251: 'The evangelist takes pains to stress the innocence of Jesus'. See 23.2, 4, 14, 22. Cf. Brown, *Death*, p. 73.

The literature familiar to Luke (and his audience) included several characters who had suffered unjustly. The most significant passage comes from Plato's *Republic*:

> ...the *just* man (ὁ δίκαιος) will have to endure the lash, the rack, chains...and finally after every extremity of suffering, he will be crucified (ἀνασχινδυλευθήσεται).[38]

Plato records the death scene of his own 'just' man in *Phaedo* 118 and focuses special attention on the final words of Socrates:

> The coldness was spreading about as far as his waist when Socrates uncovered his face, for he had covered it up, and said—*they were his last words*—Crito, we ought to offer a cock to Asclepius. See to it, and don't forget.[39]

The dying Socrates is portrayed, with his last words, as one who is pious, reverent towards the gods. One of the principal suspicions about him is effectively challenged.[40] Socrates' innocence is implicit.

Luke was similarly concerned to show that his dying subject was 'just'. And he uses the final words of Jesus—'Father, into your hands I commit my spirit'—to repudiate the suggestion that Jesus may have died forsaken by God: thus his revision of the Markan narrative.

There is, however, a more significant literary parallel of an *innocent* sufferer who dies because of his father's curse but is nevertheless reconciled to his father in his last moments. Further, it was claimed that this innocent victim was raised from the dead!

Hippolytus was renowned for his purity and his devotion to Artemis, who was regarded as a virgin goddess. Hippolytus's personal hostility towards women promoted a contempt for the indulgences of sexual pleasure. His step-mother, Phaedra, not only found him attractive but ached to enjoy sexual union with him. Hippolytus was horrified by the suggestion, and in shame and anger Phaedra committed suicide, leaving a note accusing Hippolytus of raping her.

Theseus, the father of Hippolytus, is outraged by the thought that his son has so abused Phaedra and driven her to take her life. He calls on Poseidon to destroy Hippolytus whom he banishes. The young man protests his innocence but is nevertheless fatally wounded even as he

---

38. 361E-362A (trans. P. Shorey); italics mine.

39. Trans. H. Tredennick; italics mine.

40. Cf. Plato, *Apology* 27C-E. Cf. G.W. Most, '"A Cock for Asclepius"', *Classical Quarterly* 43 (1993), p. 98.

leaves his home, entering his exile. Dying, Hippolytus is brought back to his father.

At first, Theseus rejoices in the apparent justice of his son's suffering, but Artemis herself makes known the innocence of Hippolytus. Love between father and son is restored. Although the young man dies, Artemis persuades Aesclepius to restore him to life.[41]

Several passages from Euripides' *Hippolytus* reflect themes found in Luke's passion narrative. For example, as Jesus is portrayed as suffering unjustly, so Hippolytus himself insists that he is *innocent* and does not deserve the torture he endures:

> Ah Zeus, hast thou seen? Innocent I, everfearing the gods, who was wholly heart-clean.[42]

Artemis speaks to the young man re-affirming his purity,[43] but more importantly the goddess addresses Theseus as a murderer of the holy[44] and indicates why she has revealed herself:

> I have come to show the righteousness (δικαίαν) of your son, that in fair fame he may die.[45]

She encourages Theseus to receive his son into his arms in an act of reconciliation[46] and Hippolytus himself calls out,

> Take, father, take my body and upraise.[47]

If these parallels are significant, they illustrate Luke's revision of the Markan account in order to stress the innocence of Jesus and his trust of the Father. The story of Hippolytus provided Luke with a striking model for the report of the last words and death of Jesus.

Conclusion

Both Mark and Luke, as historians, theologians, and as authors, have distinctive interests in their separate presentations. This is evident in their

---

41. See Graves, *The Greek Myths*, I, p. 358. Ovid, *Metamorphoses* 15.532ff.
42. 1363-64 (trans. A.S. Way). Cf. Lk. 23.41.
43. Cf. 1419.
44. 1287; cf. Acts 2.27.
45. 1298-99. Cf. Lk. 23.47.
46. 1431-32.
47. 1445. Cf. Lk. 23.46.

divergent accounts of the last words of Jesus.[48] Luke's purposes are more easily discerned because we are aware of his choice to depart from the Markan report.[49]

This essay has argued that Luke shaped his passion narrative in order to stress the *innocent* suffering of Jesus and in so doing was influenced by the story and character of Hippolytus, a tragic hero who unjustly endures a miserable death. Like Hippolytus, Jesus dies in the consolation that he is reconciled with his father. The words 'Father, into your hands I commit my spirit' seem to echo some of the themes in the Euripidean play and in a virtual response the centurion pronounces the certainty of Jesus' innocence.

Mark, on the other hand, wished to stress the horrifying torment of the crucifixion and Jesus' Heraclean endurance, a power that won the recognition that he was God's son. Thus, for Mark, the last words of Jesus were 'My God, my God, why have you forsaken me?' The centurion then acknowledges the divine sonship of the dead man.[50]

Despite their several and important differences, Luke and Mark both use the last words of Jesus in order to emphasize their understanding of his significance.

48. No evaluation is made of the so-called authenticity of Mark's or Luke's final words of Jesus. Both sayings have been defended as genuine: V. Taylor, *The Gospel according to St Mark* (London: Macmillan, 1955), p. 594; C.E.B. Cranfield, *The Gospel according to Saint Mark* (Cambridge: Cambridge University Press, 1963), p. 458; J.A. Fitzmyer, *The Gospel according to Luke X–XXIV* (Garden City, NY: Doubleday, 1985), p. 1513; B. Lindars, *New Testament Apologetic* (Philadelphia: Westminster, 1961), pp. 89-95.

49. Brown, *Death*, p. 1067: 'Just as at the beginning of the PN Luke omitted the passage where the Marcan Jesus began to be greatly distraught and troubled, expressing himself in the adapted language of Ps. 42.6, so at the end of the PN Luke excises the Marcan Jesus' desperate cry of abandonment...Luke's motive in this excision is primarily theological.'

50. Cf. Matera's comment, 'More forcefully than any other evangelist, Mark argues that no one can comprehend the mystery of Jesus' identity apart from his crucifixion and death on the cross': *What Are They Saying about Mark?* (New York: Paulist, 1987), p. 18.

Chapter 5

PLUTARCH AND *1 CLEMENT*

Introduction

Early Christian literature was preserved, distributed, and, it is reasonable to assume, was originally composed in the dominant language of the first and second centuries, namely Greek. The adoption of this Hellenistic foundation for the promotion of Christianity in the Roman Empire had far-reaching significance. At the very least, in using the Greek language, 'a whole world of concepts, categories of thought, inherited metaphors, and subtle connotations of meaning' came into the vocabulary and hence the thought-world of early Christianity.[1]

One of the most central themes in Greek culture was the idea of the πόλις, the so-called city-state, which was the primary political unit of ancient Greece. The πόλις was to be a constitutional government where the free citizens enjoyed political equality.[2] Thus Aristotle considers the state to be 'a sort of partnership' (κοινωνίαν) and where the desire for equality was frustrated there would be sedition.[3]

Aristotle regards the human being as, by nature, a 'political animal' (ὁ ἄνθρωπος φύσει πολιτικὸν ζῷον),[4] characterizing people as having both the impulse and the ability to form a community. According to Werner Jaeger, Aristotle was actually 'identifying *humanitas*, "being human", with the life in a state'.[5]

For the Greeks, citizenship in the πόλις not only enriched existence, it was a gift from the gods. Plato reports the origins of the πόλις in a myth attributed to Protagoras:

1.   Jaeger, *Early Christianity*, p. 6.
2.   J.-P. Vernant, *The Origins of Greek Thought* (Ithaca, NY: Cornell University Press, 1982), pp. 60-61.
3.   *Politics* 1.1.1; 5.2.1; cf. 2.4.11.
4.   *Politics* 1.1.9-10; 3.4.2.
5.   W. Jaeger, *Paideia: The Ideals of Greek Culture* (Oxford: Blackwell, 1946), I, p. 113.

Zeus therefore, fearing the total destruction of our race, sent Hermes to impart to men the qualities of respect for others and a sense of justice, so as to bring about order into our cities and create a bond of friendship and union.

Hermes asked Zeus in what manner he was to bestow these gifts on men. 'Shall I distribute them as the arts were distributed—that is, on the principle that one trained doctor suffices for many laymen, and so with the experts? Shall I distribute justice and respect for their fellows in this way or to all alike?'

'To all,' said Zeus. 'Let all have their share. There could never be cities if only a few shared in these virtues, as in the arts. Moreover, you must lay it down as my law that if anyone is incapable of acquiring his share of these two virtues he shall be put to death as a plague to the city.'[6]

In coming to the New Testament with its consistent themes of partnership/fellowship and equality within the body of Christ, it might be expected that the symbol of the city-state would offer a dynamic metaphor for the Christian community. It is startling then to find in these koine documents 'no trace at all of the aura which attended *polis*...for the Greeks'.[7]

The term πολίτευμα is found only once in the New Testament and even in this passage, Phil. 3.20, the secular, political quality of citizenship is insignificant. Rather, it is 'a figurative use of the term' referring to Christians as aliens 'in relation to the earthly sphere'. Phil. 3.20 stresses that the *heavenly* kingdom is the commonwealth to which they belong.[8]

It is only 'after' the New Testament that the state is used as a model for the church (or the kingdom of God). Significantly, it is when the congregation at Rome writes to the Corinthian community that one first finds an occurrence of the state as a metaphor for the church.[9]

The Purpose of 1 Clement

The symbolism in 1 *Clement* is dramatic. The author[10] insists on obedience to church leaders as characteristic of genuine believers. The rebellion

6. Plato, *Protagoras* 322C-D (trans. W.K.C. Guthrie).

7. H. Strathman, 'πόλις', *TDNT* 6, pp. 516-35. Cf. p. 529, 'In no passage in the NT can this translation (for πόλις) even be considered.'

8. Strathman, 'πόλις', p. 535.

9. Cf. B.E. Bowe, *A Church in Crisis* (Minneapolis, MN: Fortress Press, 1988), p. 86.

10. I will refer to the author of the epistle as Clement. Cf. Bowe, *A Church in Crisis*, p. 2.

against the Corinthian elders is regarded as 'sedition' (στάσις). This is clearly a political metaphor for their action.[11]

Yet it is not simply the 'maintenance of ecclesiastical office' that is of concern in the letter. Bowe is clearly justified in drawing attention to *1 Clem.* 63.2—the author claims to have written an 'entreaty for peace and concord' (εἰρήνης καὶ ὁμονοίας). The latter theme of concord is indeed central to Clement's message of Christian citizenship in the body of Christ.[12]

Clement writes to the community hoping to restore order: 'You therefore who laid the foundation of the sedition, submit to the presbyters and receive the correction of repentance.'[13] Clement employs 'the rules of political eloquence', calling on the Corinthians to restore harmony within the community:

> The long and powerful declarations on concord and unity in the letter of the Roman church reveal the fundamental conviction that the Christian religion, if it wants to form a true community, requires an inner discipline similar to that of the citizens of a well organized state pervaded by one spirit common to all.[14]

Jaeger concludes that Clement's impassioned, yet reasonable, epistle reveals a 'conscious philosophical reflection on the general problem involved'.[15]

Clement adopts the Hellenistic language relating to the themes of sedition and concord. There are clear and significant parallels in his letter with the orations of Dio Chrysostom and Aristides which indicate that *1 Clement* belongs to a 'common rhetorical genre'.[16]

It is the thesis of this essay that Clement's awareness of current political thought shapes his assessment of the Corinthian crisis and its needed resolution. In particular, it is fascinating to recognize the many similari-

---

11. R.M. Grant and H.H. Graham, *The Apostolic Fathers* (New York: Thomas Nelson & Sons, 1965), II, p. 17: 'Given the fact that Clement regards Christianity as a *politeia* and Christians as "citizens", it is not surprising that he condemns sedition and those who revolt.'

12. Bowe, *A Church in Crisis*, p. 23; cf. p. 86. In *1 Clement* see 9.4; 20.3, 10, 11; 21.1; 30.3; 34.7; 49.5; 50.5; 60.4; 61.1; 63.2; 65.1.

13. 57.1. Translations of *1 Clement* will largely follow the Loeb edition of Kirsopp Lake.

14. Jaeger, *Early Christianity*, pp. 13, 16-17.

15. Jaeger, *Early Christianity*, pp. 17-18.

16. Bowe, *A Church in Crisis*, p. 86.

ties between the letter and Plutarch's *Praecepta Gerendae Reipublicae*. In language and intention Clement reveals a deep familiarity with Plutarch's 'precepts of statesmanship'.[17] I do not argue for literary dependence; it is sufficient to be alert to the parallels.

Plutarch's Praecepta Gerendae Reipublicae

Plutarch's Political Writings

> I need to be allowed to give attention to the signs of the soul in persons and so illustrate the life of each, leaving to others the accounts of their great achievements.[18]

In several respects, by modern standards, Plutarch's *Lives* cannot be regarded as strict historiography. Rather than reporting important events, Plutarch's 'special concern' is with the character, the signs of the soul, of the individuals he describes. Indeed, the political virtue of these figures is of critical significance for Plutarch. The πολιτικός will be concerned primarily 'to create or maintain the right conditions in which the community will prosper'.[19] Thus Plutarch praises Pericles for his πολιτείαν because it was exercised in the best interests of the welfare of all.[20] Similarly, Plutarch comments that Thales' poetry was effective politically, inspiring people to renounce their factionalism. They then 'dwelt together in a common search for what was lofty and noble'.[21]

Plutarch's concern for harmony in the political community is the particular focus of his treatise *Praecepta Gerendae Reipublicae* where he outlines the responsibilities of the πολιτικός:

> ...the statesman, if he cannot keep the State entirely free from troubles, will at any rate try to cure and control whatever disturbs it and causes sedition (στασιάζον)...
> ...the best thing is to see to it in advance that factional discord shall never arise (μηδέποτε στασιάζωσι) among them and to regard this as the greatest and the noblest function of what may be called the art of statesmanship.[22]

17. Cf. Jones, *Plutarch and Rome*, pp. 117-19.
18. Plutarch, *Alex.* 1.3.
19. A. Wardman, *Plutarch's Lives* (Berkeley, CA: University of California Press, 1974), pp. 1, 49-50, 57.
20. Plutarch, *Per.* 15.2.
21. Plutarch, *Lyc.* 4.2.
22. Cf. Xenophon, *Memorabilia* 4.2.2.

...There remains, then, of those activities which fall within the statesman's province, only this—and it is equal to any of the other blessings—
always to instil concord and friendship in those who dwell together and to
remove strifes, discords, and all enmity.[23]

Surely this is an accurate description of Clement's purpose in writing.
He is primarily motivated to end any sedition and to promote harmony
within the community:[24]

For you will give us joy and gladness, if you are obedient to the things
that we have written through the Holy Spirit, and root out the wicked
passion of your jealousy according to the entreaty for peace and concord
which we have made in this letter.

Send back quickly to us our messengers Claudius Ephebus and
Valerius Vito and Fortunatus, in peace with gladness, in order that they
may report the sooner the peace and concord which we pray for and
desire, that we also may the more speedily rejoice in your good order.[25]

Parallels with 1 Clement

Plutarch insists that the πολιτικὸς ought to be alert to the character
(ἤθους) of the community.[26] It is striking that Clement gives immediate
attention to the reputation and (former) virtue of the Corinthian congregation: 'Who has not admired the sobriety and Christian gentleness of
your piety? Who has not reported your ἤθος so magnificent in its
hospitality?'[27] For Clement, the significance of hospitality is shown in
that it is a clear, visible demonstration of genuine faith.[28]

As Plutarch outlines his precepts for the πολιτικὸς he chooses to
focus on the political virtue of hospitality:

...the good person...the one who is prudent is...affable and generally
accessible and approachable for all, keeping a house always unlocked as a
harbour of refuge for those in need, and showing solicitude and friendli-
ness, not only by acts of service, but also by sharing the griefs of those
who fail and the joy of those who succeed.[29]

23. *Praecepta* 815B; 824B-D. The translation largely follows H.N. Fowler's in
the Loeb edition.
24. For 'sedition' and related terms see *1 Clem.* 1.1; 2.6; 3.2; 4.12; 14.2; 43.2;
46.7, 9; 47.6; 49.5; 51.1, 3; 54.2; 55.1; 57.1; 63.1.
25. *1 Clem.* 63.2; 65.1.
26. *Praecepta* 799B.
27. *1 Clem.* 1.2.
28. *1 Clem.* 10.7; 11.1; 12.1. Cf. Garrison, *Redemptive Almsgiving*, pp. 81-82.
29. *Praecepta* 823A.

Plutarch, in his concern for the well-being of the political community, maintains great respect both for public office and for the individuals who held such positions:

> ...deeming every public office to be something great and sacred, we must pay the highest honour to one who holds an office; but the honour of an office resides in concord and friendship with one's colleagues much more than in crowns and a purple-bordered robe.
>
> ...how can anyone be considered honorable and fair-minded who detracts from the dignity of a colleague in office, or maliciously flouts that colleague with actions which reveal ambitious rivalry, being so self-willed (αὐθαδείας) as to arrogate and to annex everything to oneself at the expense of a colleague?[30]

For Clement, those who have brought about the rebellion in the Corinthian church are described as 'self-willed' (αὐθάδη) and he was certainly provoked to write his letter because of the removal of certain elders from their office. With obvious indignation he writes:

> It is a shameful report, beloved, extremely shameful, and unworthy of your training in Christ, that on account of one or two persons the stedfast and ancient church of the Corinthians is being disloyal to the presbyters.[31]
>
> ...it is not just to remove from their ministry those who were appointed by them [i.e., the apostles], or later on by other eminent persons, with the consent of the whole Church...in spite of their good service you have removed some from the ministry which they fulfilled blamelessly.[32]

Because of the Corinthian revolt against the elders, Clement insists on the need for repentance. 'You therefore, who laid the foundation of the sedition, submit to the presbyters, and receive the correction of μετάνοιαν bending the knees of your hearts.'[33]

Clement carefully weaves praise of the Corinthian Christians' reputation with a harsh indictment of their treatment of the presbyters, summoning the congregation to repentance. The boldness of the letter is inspired by his 'political' objective of restoring concord. Again Plutarch offers an intriguing parallel:

> For blame which is mingled with praise and contains nothing insulting but merely frankness of speech, and arouses not anger but a pricking

---

30. *Praecepta* 816A, C-D.
31. *1 Clem.* 47.6.
32. *1 Clem.* 44.3, 6.
33. *1 Clem.* 57.1; repentance is a central theme in the letter (cf. 7.4–8.5; 62.2).

of the conscience and repentance (μετάνοιαν), appears both kindly and healing.[34]

Ultimately Clement hopes to return harmony and unity to the church by encouraging a mutual respect and love between individual members of the community. Even while he is an advocate for the 'wronged' elders, Clement seeks to promote equality and justice for all parts of the body:

> For the great cannot exist without the small, nor the small without the great. Every organism is composed of various different elements; and this ensures its own good. Take the body as an instance; the head is nothing without the feet, nor are the feet anything without the head. Even the smallest of our physical members are necessary and valuable to the whole body; yet all of them work together, united in a common subordination, to preserve the whole body.
>
> In Christ Jesus, then, let this corporate body of ours be likewise maintained, with each of us giving way to our neighbor in proportion to our spiritual gifts. The strong are to care for the weak, and the weak are to respect the strong. The rich should provide for the poor and the poor should thank God for giving them somebody to supply their needs.[35]

Plutarch shares this concern for equality within the community. In outlining the responsibilities and objectives of the πολιτικὸς Plutarch makes the following statements:

> The statesman should soothe the ordinary citizens by granting them equality and the powerful by concessions in return.
>
> One ought to conciliate superiors, add prestige to inferiors, honor equals, and be affable and friendly to all.
>
> …in the matter of power the low-born should be made equal to the nobles, the poor to the rich, and the private citizen to the office-holders.[36]

Conclusion

It is not surprising that a Christian document written in Greek would adopt the metaphor of the 'state' for the church. What is unusual is that the New Testament does *not* offer this interpretation. This symbolism is first encountered in the Apostolic Fathers.

First Clement is best interpreted not merely as a piece of early

---

34. *Praecepta* 810C.
35. *1 Clem.* 37.4–38.2.
36. *Praecepta* 815A; 816B; 821C-D.

Christian literature addressing ecclesiological issues but as a politically inspired letter seeking, through the forms of Hellenistic rhetoric, to restore concord to a community ravaged by sedition. The author is very familiar with the 'precepts (written and unwritten) of statesmanship' current in his own culture, Rome in the late first century.

Chapter 6

LEGIONS OF ANGELS AND THE WILL OF GOD

Introduction

As Paul outlined the theological foundation for the idea of election or predestination he asked rhetorically, 'Why does God find fault with anyone? For who can resist his will?' (Rom. 9.19). The implication seems to be that the βουλή of God determines 'fate'. How, then, is one to understand the θέλημα of God in relation to the divine purpose that is irresistible?[1] Although this serious question deserves attention, a broader concern is addressed in the present essay, focusing on Matthew's portrait of Jesus as confronting the will of God.

When Jesus was arrested in the Garden of Gethsemane, someone, in an attempt to defend him, drew a sword and struck the slave of the high priest.

> Then Jesus said to him, 'Put your sword back into its place; for all who take the sword will perish by the sword. Do you think that I cannot appeal to my Father, and he will at once send me more than twelve legions of angels? But how then would the scriptures be fulfilled which say it must happen this way?' (Mt. 26.52-54).

The theme of fulfilling the scriptures is very prominent in the Gospel tradition, especially in Matthew,[2] and is virtually synonymous with accomplishing the will of God. Thus as John reports the incident in Gethsemane he writes that Jesus said to the swordsman (who is identified as Peter), 'Put your sword back into its sheath. Am I not to drink the cup that the Father has given me?' (Jn 18.11)

In exploring this passage, one of the central themes to be considered is

---

1.   This question is particularly relevant in light of Lk. 22.42. Among the authors of the Gospels, the phrase 'the βουλή of God' appears to be confined to the writings of Luke (Lk. 7.30; Acts 2.23; 13.36; 20.27). However, see Mt. 11.27 = Lk. 10.22.

2.   Mt. 1.22; 2.15, 17, 23; 4.14; 8.17; 12.17; 13.14, 35; 21.4; 26.54, 56; 27.9.

the perceived role of fate in shaping the events of Jesus' life and death. Does the will of God determine what will take place or does Jesus freely choose to fulfil a 'fate' that is in fact optional?

In seeking to understand how Matthew (and Jesus) regarded the significance of voluntarily doing God's will, attention will be given to the characters of Achilles, Socrates, and Ignatius of Antioch as each came to accept death as their 'fate'.

A Choice of Fates: Achilles

In Homer's *Iliad*, Achilles, the hero of the Trojan War, is warned by his divine mother (Thetis) that one of two fates will be his: either he will die in the battle and win glory for himself, or else forsaking the fight he will return to Greece and live a long but obscure life. The choice between these 'fates' is his.[3]

In a fit of jealousy, rivalry, and vanity, which culminates in the virtual theft of his female captive, Achilles becomes enraged at Agamemnon, the commander of the army. Achilles prepares to return to Greece. When the mighty hero refuses to enter the fight with the Trojans, Achilles' dearest friend Patrocles takes up Achilles' armour and marches onto the battlefield. Although victorious through much of the struggle, Patrocles is eventually killed by the Trojan champion Hector. When Achilles learns of his comrade's death, he is driven by grief to seek revenge even if he must embrace the 'fate' that will lead to his own early loss of life. Thetis warns Achilles but he chooses to kill Hector though he himself will die:[4]

> Thetis cried out through her tears, 'From what you say, you're doomed to a short life, my son! For shortly after Hector's death your own must come.'
>   In despair[5] Achilles responded, 'Then let me die quickly since it was not my fate to save my closest friend from his death.'[6]

Achilles accepts the possibility, even the inevitability, of his death and finds consolation in the example of Heracles:

> Now I will go out to attack Hector himself, the man who killed the one I loved. I will accept my fate whenever Zeus and the other immortal gods will to bring it to pass. The powerful Heracles did not escape death even

3.   *Iliad* 9.410ff.

4.   For the Socratic or Platonic interpretation see Plato's *Apology* 28B-D.

5.   For an interesting parallel, see the 'despair' of Jesus in Gethsemane, Mk 14.33-34.

6.   *Iliad* 18.94-99.

though he was dear to Zeus...Fate and the horrible wrath of Hera over-
came him. So also will I, if a similar fate awaits me, lie low in death. But
now let me win glorious fame...[7]

Achilles, then, is the heroic example of the individual who is aware of a
choice of 'fates' and nevertheless dares knowingly to select the path that
leads to a premature death.[8]

Recognizing Fate: Socrates

Xenophon's portrait of Socrates indicates that the latter regarded his
death as willed by God (= the gods) and that he accepted the verdict at
his trial. Plato basically confirms this. Recognizing his 'fate', Socrates
considered his death a blessing.

Xenophon describes Socrates as gladly accepting the sentence of
death because God apparently understood it to be superior to the slow
physical and intellectual decay of advancing years of life.[9] Indeed,
Xenophon regards the execution of Socrates as a 'god-loved fate'
(θεοφιλοῦς μοίρας).[10]

Socrates 'was persuaded that the moment had come for him to die'.[11]
This realization had come partially through the experience at his trial
when the gods opposed his development of a strategic defence.[12] Further,
he believed that God's will would be reflected through the jury's
verdict.[13] Socrates' final words in Plato's *Crito* well represent this
attitude: 'God leads us in this way'.[14]

Socrates, then, represents the individual who recognizes the will of
God even in his death.

Determining Fate: Ignatius of Antioch

Ignatius was an early Christian, the bishop of Antioch, martyred late in
the reign of Trajan (98–117 CE). It was his conviction that in dying he

7.   *Iliad* 18.115-21.
8.   On Achilles' choice of 'fates', cf. Lucian, *The Patriot* 15.
9.   Xenophon, *Apology* 5; 7; 9.
10.   Xenophon, *Apology* 32. Cf. Plato, *Apology* 19A: 'Let this be as God wills'
(τῷ θεῷ φίλον); *Crito* 43D: 'If this is the will of the gods, then let this be' (τοῖς
θεοῖς φίλον).
11.   Xenophon, *Apology* 22.
12.   Xenophon, *Apology* 8.
13.   Cf. Xenophon, *Apology* 7; Plato, *Apology* 35D-E.
14.   Plato, *Crito* 54E.

would become a true disciple[15] and that martyrdom was his 'lot'.[16] The use of this term implies that Ignatius regarded his execution to be predestined, a God-given 'fate'.[17]

While believing that his death was fore-ordained, Ignatius nevertheless desperately sought to prevent the Roman Christians, regardless of their motives, from intervening with the authorities to rescue him from martyrdom. He was convinced that they might prevent his being martyred and take away his opportunity to share in Christ's suffering:[18]

> ...provided that I attain the grace to receive my fate without interference. For I am afraid of your love, in that it may do me wrong; for it is easy for you to do what you want, but it is difficult for me to reach God, unless you spare me...[19]

> I am writing to all the churches and I command everyone that I am dying willingly for God, if you do not prevent it.

> Even if I beg you myself, do not be persuaded; instead obey this that I write: for in the midst of life I desire death.

> I have no desire to live like other people and [my death] shall come about if you desire it. Desire it...[20]

Ignatius apparently was granted his hope to die for God.[21] It is reasonable, then, to regard his actions as determining fate.

Each of these individuals—Achilles, Socrates, and Ignatius—preferred a 'fate' which brought a premature death. In the motivations and convictions of each are important elements which are also found in Matthew's portrait of Jesus. Jesus exhibits the heroism of Achilles, the insight and commitment of Socrates, and the deliberate, even calculating, determination of Ignatius.

---

15. E.g., Ignatius, *Eph.* 3.1-2; *Rom.* 4.2-3.

16. κλῆρος, Ignatius, *Trall.* 12.3; *Rom.* 1.2.

17. W. Foerster, 'κλῆρος', *TDNT* 3 (1965), p. 763; Cf. *Mart. Pol.* 6.2. For a striking statement regarding martyrdom and the will of God see *Mart. Pol.* 2.1; cf. 7.1.

18. Ignatius, *Rom.* 6.3 (cf. 6.1); *Magn.* 5.2.

19. Ignatius, *Rom.* 1.2b (trans. J.B. Lightfoot and J.R. Harmer).

20. Ignatius, *Rom.* 4.1; 7.2; 8.1. Cf. K. Lake (ed.), *The Apostolic Fathers* (Cambridge, MA: Harvard University Press, 1976), I, pp. 166-67.

21. For the likelihood of Ignatius's martyrdom see W.R. Schoedel, *Ignatius of Antioch* (Philadelphia: Fortress Press, 1985), p. 11.

Matthew and the 'Fate' of Jesus

The tradition of the Gospels consistently regards the death of Jesus, however tragic and unjust, as nevertheless the will of God. Indeed, John seems to be deterministic in regarding the crucifixion of Jesus as foreordained, even 'commanded by God'.[22] Luke apparently holds a similar view as evidenced by his changing of 'the Son of man goes as it is written of him' to 'the Son of man[23] is going as it has been determined'.[24] Matthew, however, regards the fulfilment of the scriptures as in some way both shaped by God himself and yet voluntarily completed by human beings.[25] Thus after acknowledging that another course of action was available to him (namely, calling on the help of twelve legions of angels), Jesus remarks 'But how then should the scriptures be fulfilled that it must be so?' (Mt. 26.54).

Indeed, Matthew understands the specific mission, the purpose, of Jesus' coming to be in order to fulfil the sacred writings. Early in the Gospel, Jesus says, 'Do not think that I have come to abolish the law and the prophets; I have come not to abolish but to fulfill' (Mt. 5.17).

The Will of God in Matthew

In Matthew's Gospel, the familial intimacy of the disciples to Jesus is understood as a measure of how well they perform the will of God.

> For whoever does the will of my Father in heaven is my brother, and sister, and mother.[26]

22. Jn 12.27; 14.31. Cf. W.R. Wilson, *The Execution of Jesus* (New York: Charles Scribner's Sons, 1970), p. 64.

23. Perhaps there was early widespread tradition concerning the scriptural expectation that the *Son of Man* was to suffer, die, and rise from death (Mk 8.31 = Lk. 9.22: Matthew omits the Son of man reference in 16.21; Mk 9.12, also omitted by Matthew in 16.11 though v. 12 suggests his awareness; Lk. 24.6, 7; Jn 3.14; 12.34).

24. Mk 14.21; Lk. 22.22. Thus the death of Jesus is 'according to what has been determined (by God), according to the counsel (of God)' K.L. Schmidt, 'ὁρίζω', *TDNT*, V, p. 452. Luke's perspective is well expressed in 24.44, words of the risen Christ: '...everything written about me in the law of Moses and the prophets and the psalms must (δεῖ) be fulfilled.'

25. So also, for Matthew it is important to pray that God's will be accomplished on earth (6.10). This petition is absent in Luke.

26. Mt. 12.50. Matthew apparently inherited this from Mk 3.35 and modified it ('my Father' rather than 'God'). Luke, significantly, reports the saying as 'My mother and my brothers are those who hear the word of God and do it' (8.21), thus

This evaluation of discipleship determines whether an individual will enter the kingdom of heaven. Neither Christology nor the ability, by invoking the name of Jesus, to achieve mighty works will be a sufficient prerequisite for entrance.[27]

In contrast to the religious leaders who merely praise God with their lips,[28] the followers of Jesus, the genuine disciples, are to be characterized by a humble repentance that prompts them to fulfil the will of God in their actions and so demonstrate that they are truly God's children.

> What do you think? A man had two sons and going to the first he said, 'Go work in the vineyard today, Son.' And he answered, 'I will not' but later changed his mind and went. Going to the other he said the same. He answered, 'Sir, I will'. Yet he did not go. Which of the two did the will of the father?[29]

Surely, if the disciple is expected to perform the will of God, nothing less is to be anticipated in the example of Jesus.[30] And as the followers are to pray that God's will be done, so Jesus accepts his Father's θέλημα, forsaking his own.[31]

The Coming Death of Jesus

It was early Christianity's conviction that in accepting death Jesus submitted to the will of God. Indeed, the cross represents the purpose and climax of the life and ministry of Jesus. Even in reporting the Infancy Narrative, Matthew seems to draw attention to the eventual death of his protagonist.

It is the exalted status of the baby that puts Jesus at risk. Similarly, when he was an adult Jesus would confront the defiant disbelief of those who would say 'What authority do you have for doing these things and who gave you such authority?' (Mt. 21.23). When the child is designated 'king of the Jews'[32] by the magi, the title apparently provokes a hostile

avoiding a reference to the will of God. Cf. *2 Clem.* 9.11.

27. Mt. 7.21-23; peculiar to Matthew. Cf. Lk. 6.46; see *2 Clem.* 4.1-3.

28. Cf. Mt. 15.1-9.

29. Mt. 21.28-31a; peculiar to Matthew.

30. Cf. Mt. 10.24-25a.

31. Mt. 6.10; 26.39, 42. It is worth noting that Matthew draws attention to the words of Jesus in the repeated prayer, using a phrase that echoes 6.10. This interest is not apparent in the parallels.

32. ὁ τεχθεὶς βασιλεὺς τῶν Ἰουδαίων, 2.2.

response from Herod, the ostensible king of the Jews.[33] This appellation for Jesus not only sparked Herod's wrath; Roman power was also threatened by the messianic hope implicit in the reference to Jewish royalty. Thus, according to Matthew, Pontius Pilate's first question to the adult Jesus was, 'Are you the king of the Jews?[34] and significantly, the charge against Jesus placed on the cross read 'This is Jesus the king of the Jews'.[35]

Following the Infancy Narrative, Matthew focuses exclusively on the adult Jesus and his ministry. No longer choosing to foreshadow the death of Jesus, the author indicates that the approach of a violent end was obvious to Jesus, even recognized as necessary.

According to Matthew, Jesus regarded the typical destiny of prophets to be one of persecution and martyrdom. The disciples were to feel privileged to share their 'calling'.[36] Although John the Baptist was 'more than a prophet',[37] he too suffered a violent death and Jesus expected, as the Son of Man, to meet a similar 'fate' (Mt. 17.12-13). Thus, Jesus anticipated his prophet-like murder at the hands of the tenants of the vineyard.[38] Consequently, the Matthean Jesus speaks of the inevitability that the Son of Man suffer and die.[39]

In his expectation that he, like the prophets before him, would be put to death, Jesus believed that the scriptures 'foretold' the necessity of his suffering and dying. Inasmuch as he was convinced of their scriptural certainty, Jesus regarded his coming trial and execution to be the will of God. Thus, he was eager to have the writings 'fulfilled'.[40] Even though Jesus thought he had the *right* to avoid arrest by calling on his Father's assistance with twelve legions of angels,[41] Jesus chose to fulfil the scriptures and the will of God by allowing himself to be taken by the crowd.[42]

33. Cf. Mt. 2.1.
34. ὁ βασιλεὺς τῶν Ἰουδαίων, 27.11.
35. ὁ βασιλεὺς τῶν Ἰουδαίων, 27.37. See Brown, *Death*, I, p. 717.
36. Mt. 5.12; cf. 10.40-42; 23.29-37.
37. περισσότερον προφήτου, 11.9; cf. 21.26.
38. Mt. 21.33-41; cf. 13.57; 16.13-14; 21.11, 46.
39. Mt. 17.22-23; 20.17-19; 26.24; cf. 16.21 where the Son of Man reference is lacking; 12.40; 17.9, 12.
40. Mt. 26.54; cf. 26.31, 56.
41. '*He will at once send* (them)', Mt. 26.53.
42. Cf. Wilson, *Execution*, p. 48.

Jesus, Achilles, Socrates, Ignatius, and 'Fate'

As Achilles was aware that a certain course of action would lead to the 'fate' of an early death, so Jesus was alert to the danger of continuing his ministry. Achilles nevertheless chose the path that would soon bring about his loss of life; he did not embrace the opportunity to escape. Similarly, Jesus could have avoided his arrest and execution by calling on twelve legions of angels but instead deliberately pursued a course of action that would precipitate his premature death.

Jesus, in Matthew's Gospel, heroically embraced the more difficult 'fate'. He voluntarily submitted to the will of God as outlined in the scriptures which describe the violent end of several of the prophets.[43] Like Achilles, Jesus consciously, deliberately, and willingly chose to give up his life.

The representation of Socrates as recognizing that his death was a 'fate' willed by God (= the gods) is strikingly similar to the Gospel portrait of Jesus as accepting God's intention for him to die. As Socrates made no serious attempt to win acquittal at his trial, so Jesus, convinced of God's will, offered virtually no defence at his interrogation before Pilate (Mt. 27.12-14).

As Ignatius, bishop of Antioch, sought to arrange (orchestrate?) circumstances in order to ensure and so achieve his 'God-willed' martyrdom, so Jesus chose not to escape death by appealing for the assistance of twelve legions of angels. Jesus was apparently driven by the conviction that the scriptures must be fulfilled and that his death was one of the events prophesied.

While submitting voluntarily to the long-term plan of God, Jesus apparently recognized and chose to accept the immediate requirements of God's will as they facilitated the fulfilment of that plan. This may represent a 'middle position' in the conflict involving predestination and free will and may leave many questions unanswered. It is, however, the best way to understand the claim of the Matthean Jesus that he could call on twelve legions of angels in order to avoid being arrested.

---

43. See 2 Chron. 36.15-16.

Chapter 7

THE LOVE OF MONEY IN POLYCARP'S LETTER TO THE PHILIPPIANS

> Don't you know[1] that to be covetous of either honour or money[2] is not
> only said to be, it really is, a reproach?[3]

Plato insisted that the truly good man would use his riches for noble
purposes—for the good of the polis—and not seek merely to compound
his wealth. Thus it was commonly believed that money should be used,
not simply stockpiled. Avarice and greed were repudiated, but a reasonable, and self-controlled, mastery of possessions was considered healthy.[4]

Plato and Aristotle regarded the love of money to be a characteristic
inappropriate for the good man.[5] Consequently, φιλαργυρία came to be
considered one of the 'classic vices of Hellenistic moral philosophy'.[6]
Love of money came to be condemned as a virtual source or breeding
ground of multiple evils.[7] In the first century BCE, Cicero maintained
that the most glaring and reprehensible feature of a selfish person was
the passion for wealth:

> There is nothing more honourable and noble than to be indifferent to money
> if one does not possess it and to devote it to beneficence and liberality if
> one does possess it.[8]

---

1. ἢ οὐκ οἶσθα; cf. 1 Cor. 6.2, 3, 9, 15, 16, 19.
2. φιλάργυρον.
3. Plato, *Republic* 347B.
4. Cf. Isocrates, *Demonicus*, 27.
5. Plato, *Republic* 347B; Aristotle, *Politics* 2.6.20.
6. L.T. Johnson, *Sharing Possessions* (Philadelphia: Fortress Press, 1980),
p. 119.
7. Cf. Diogenes Laertius 6.50: 'The love of money (Diogenes) regarded as the
metropolis (μητρόπολιν) of all evils.'
8. Cicero, *On Duty* 1.20.68 (trans. W. Miller). Plutarch describes the love of
money as a 'disease of the soul', *Concerning Talkativeness* 502E.

The Hellenistic perspective of the author of the Pastoral Epistles embraces this principle. Thus, 'love of money' is condemned as a wicked vice which will be a common attribute of people in the last days; it is the root of all evils.[9] Having denounced this sin and its deadly potential,[10] the author advises those community members who are wealthy to make wise use of their resources:

> Concerning those who are rich in this age: Admonish them not to be haughty nor to base their hopes on uncertain wealth but on God who richly provides us everything to enjoy. They are to *do good*,[11] to be rich in good deeds, both liberal and sharing, so laying a good foundation for their future, so that they may receive the life which is genuine (1 Tim. 6.17-19).

When Polycarp wrote to the Christian community in Philippi in the first half of the second century, he echoed several of these concerns about wealth and the love of money. As well as being apprehensive about the specific dangers of this vice, Polycarp employs the emerging doctrine of redemptive almsgiving to call the congregation to generosity and mutual love.

In Polycarp's letter to the Philippian church he warns the community to avoid the love of money (φιλαργυρίας) and instead to 'love the things that God loved' (*Phil.* 2.2). Polycarp returns to this theme in the fourth chapter, cautioning his readers deliberately to remove themselves from the love of money insisting that it is the 'beginning of all evils' (ἀρχὴ...χαλεπῶν).[12] Valens, the fallen presbyter, was apparently a victim of such greed (*Phil.* 11.1-4).

Polycarp was bishop of Smyrna during the first half of the second century and wrote to the Philippian community shortly after the visit of Ignatius. His purpose was to provide a 'covering letter' for the copies of Ignatius's epistles he was sending to that church, although Polycarp certainly addresses other issues.

It has been argued that the epistle of Polycarp to the Philippians in its present form is in fact two letters 'fused into one', the first comprising ch. 13 (and perhaps 14), the second being made up of the first twelve

---

9.   2 Tim. 3.1-2; 1 Tim. 6.10.
10.   Cf. Mk 4.19.
11.   ἀγαθοεργεῖν. See n. 29.
12.   *Phil.* 4.1, 3; 6.1; For the translation of χαλεπῶν as 'evils' see *Mart. Pol.* 11.1; *Herm. Man.* 6.2.10.

chapters.[13] The primary basis for such a conjecture is that in ch. 9, Polycarp apparently regards Ignatius as dead, having been martyred: '...Ignatius...did not run in vain... (he is) with the Lord' (9.1-2). Yet in ch. 13, Polycarp asks his readers for any recent information they may have about Ignatius and his companions, implying that they are not yet dead.[14]

Lightfoot defended the integrity of the extant epistle and maintained that the reference to 'those who *are* with' Ignatius is due to the error of the Latin translator. According to Lightfoot, the original Greek probably read τοῖς σὺν αὐτῷ or perhaps τοῖς μετ' αὐτοῦ, leaving the tense ambiguous. Polycarp's interest then would have been in any information about Ignatius and his companions prior to their deaths. It would be assumed that they had been killed, that they were 'with the Lord'.[15]

Others have assumed the unity of the letter and argued that Ignatius was, in fact, alive when it was written. With reference to the passage in ch. 9 the casual suggestion is made that Polycarp regarded 'Ignatius' zeal for martyrdom as certain to achieve its goal'.[16]

For our purposes, the issue can remain unresolved. There is virtually no reason to doubt the genuineness of the extant epistle to the Philippians as the work of Polycarp. This much is not in dispute. Consequently, any evidence this writing may provide for the belief in redemptive almsgiving[17] is relevant to a study of the doctrine in early Christianity during the period 70–135 CE

Polycarp's letter to the Philippians abounds with allusions to, and citations from, the New Testament. As might be expected, Polycarp maintains the traditional early Christian soteriology, namely, that Jesus died for people's sins.[18] At the same time, however, within the letter there is also an emphasis on brotherly love and compassion for the needy, as well as a harsh repudiation of the love of money.

The bishop of Smyrna opens his letter by immediately commending the Philippians for their hospitality. The virtue praised by the New

13. P.N. Harrison, *Polycarp's Two Epistles to the Philippians* (Cambridge: Cambridge University Press, 1936), p. 15.

14. *Phil.* 13.2d; this portion of the verse is known only in its Latin form.

15. J.B. Lightfoot, *The Apostolic Fathers* (Grand Rapids, MI: Baker, 1981), II.1, pp. 578, 588-89.

16. E.J. Goodspeed, *A History of Early Christian Literature* (Chicago: University of Chicago Press, 1966), p. 17.

17. See Garrison, *Redemptive Almsgiving*.

18. *Phil.* 1.2; 8.1.

Testament, Clement, and Hermas is of equal significance to Polycarp. As Clement begins his letter acknowledging and complimenting the Corinthians' reputation for hospitality, so Polycarp is enthusiastic in greeting the Philippians. He finds joy because they 'followed the pattern of *true love*' in ministering to those saints who were in chains as they passed through the city.[19]

Like Clement, Polycarp recognizes love as the highest virtue. Love of God, love of Christ, and love of neighbour have precedence in the Christian faith;[20] love fulfils 'the command of righteousness'.[21] He adds the striking comment that the one who has love is far from all sin.[22] This passage could be interpreted to mean that love covers sin and distances the individual from his guilt; it is more likely, however, that Polycarp means that the one who acts in love rarely falls into sin. He then goes on to write about those sins which are incompatible with the life of faith and love. Chief among these deeds is the love of money; it is the source of all evils.[23] Indeed, Polycarp deliberately contrasts two claims:

1. the one who has love is far from all sin;
2. the beginning of all evils is the love of money.

Polycarp's letter consistently stresses that Christians must not be worldly. Not only must they be free from the love of money, but they should not 'love this present world' (*Phil.* 9.2). Further, 'it is good to be cut off from the lusts of the world' (*Phil.* 5.3). Significantly, a true disregard for wealth is demonstrated through generous giving. Thus, after one injunction to refrain from the love of money, Polycarp goes on to quote the words of Jesus: 'Be merciful that you may obtain mercy; with the measure you give, it shall be measured to you again'.[24] Charity shall be rewarded. The Philippians are encouraged to ensure that they will receive reciprocal mercy for their deeds of kindness. This has added

---

19. *1 Clem.* 1.2-3; *Phil.* 1.1. Note the comments of Clement of Alexandria regarding hospitality, *Strom.* 2.9: 'akin to love is hospitality, being a congenial art devoted to the treatment of strangers... Hospitality is therefore occupied in what is useful for strangers, and guests are strangers and friends are guests and brethren are friends... If the real man within us is the spiritual, philanthropy is brotherly love to those who participate in the same spirit.'

20. προαγούσης.

21. *Phil.* 3.3; cf. Paul in Rom. 13.9-10 and Gal. 5.14; and Mt. 22.34-40.

22. *Phil.* 3.3; cf. Ignatius, *Eph.* 14.2.

23. ἀρχή, 4.1; see 2.2; 4.3; 5.2; 6.1.

24. *Phil.* 2.2-3; cf. *1 Clem.* 13.1-2.

force as Polycarp warns that 'we must all appear before the judgment seat of Christ and each must give an account of himself' (*Phil.* 6.2).

As Ignatius had instructed Polycarp to protect the widows and to see that their needs were met,[25] so Polycarp regards widows as an altar of God.[26] This metaphor is developed in later sources,[27] but even here the implication is that sacrifices are brought to the altar. The symbolism requires almsgiving to be regarded as a sacrifice.[28] Here was the clear evidence of love and a disdain for wealth. As might be expected, Polycarp advocates the meritorious power of almsgiving:

> Stand fast, therefore, in these things and follow the example of the Lord, firm and unchangeable in faith, loving the brotherhood, affectionate to one another, joined together in the truth forestalling one another in the gentleness of the Lord, despising no man. When you can do good,[29] do not delay, for almsgiving sets free from death. Be subject one to another, having your manner of life blameless among the Gentiles that you may receive praise for your good works and that the Lord may not be blasphemed in you (*Phil.* 10.1-2).

Love for fellow believers and freedom from the love of money are both expressed through almsgiving. Giving to the needy, despising no man,[30] demonstrates a genuine love for neighbour. It is clear proof that one is not 'lusting after the world' and it is a witness to the unbeliever who will praise this good work. In turn the Lord is honoured and the giver of alms will find mercy before the judgment seat of God.

Polycarp shows some preference for the LXX version of Proverbs in stating his concern for the needy. The influence of Prov. 3.27 (which may have shaped Ecclus. 29.8-9 as well) is apparent: 'Do not refrain from doing good to the poor when your hand is able to help.' Further, Polycarp adapts the LXX form of Prov. 3.4 when he instructs the elders:

> Be compassionate, merciful to all. Bring back those who have wandered, caring for all the weak, neglecting neither widow, nor orphan, nor poor, but 'ever providing for that which is good before God and man' (*Phil.* 6.1).

25. Ignatius, *Pol.* 4.1.
26. θυσιαστήριον, 4.3.
27. Cf. *Apostolic Constitutions* (Funk's division) 3.12.1-2; 3.14.1; Didascalia 3.6.
28. Cf. Heb. 13.16; also *Herm. Sim.* 5.3.7-8.
29. 'Do good' as a synonym for charity: cf. Mk 14.7; Lk. 6.33-35; 1 Tim. 6.18; Heb. 13.16; *Herm. Man.* 2.4; *Herm. Vis.* 3.9.5; Clement of Alexandria, *Rich Man* 33; *Paed.* 3.7 (see also Gal. 6.9-10).
30. Cf. the textual variant of Lk. 6.35.

It is likely then that Polycarp was familiar with Prov. 15.27 in the LXX. In some way, good works, including charity and 'being far from all love of money', are motivated by the knowledge that *every man owes the debt of sin (Phil. 6.1)*. Presumably, Polycarp is anxious for the redemption of *post-baptismal* sin. Almsgiving is central to his remedy.

Polycarp clearly regards almsgiving, charity to the poor, as a duty of love that is demanded by Proverbs and by the words of Jesus. Almsgiving is an act of compassion, an act of kindness that warrants reciprocal mercy from God. It will be rewarded; perhaps it is even redemptive. A significant feature of almsgiving is that it shows one is free from the love of money.

Polycarp indicates that the principal sin of Valens, the fallen elder, was avarice. His love of money corrupted him and Polycarp takes the opportunity to warn his readers of the dangers of greed (*Phil. 11.1-2*). Here is a stark contrast to selfless almsgiving, and it might be asked whether Valens had been guilty of misappropriating the alms he was to distribute for the congregation. Such a conjecture is reasonable but beyond being substantiated. What is clear, however, is that Polycarp explicitly teaches that almsgiving rescues from death. He endorses the doctrine found in Tobit.

While it is uncertain whether a doctrine of redemptive almsgiving is to be found in the New Testament—the evidence is not conclusive—it is undeniable that during the period 70–135 CE in early Christianity the view clearly emerges that charity to the poor, particularly in the form of alms, is of great spiritual benefit to the one who gives. Thus Polycarp, who condemns the love of money, prompts generosity when he writes, 'When you can do good do not delay, for almsgiving sets free from death'. Polycarp adapts the Hellenistic attitude toward φιλαργυρία which is reflected in the New Testament but in affirming it also stresses that the act of almsgiving is redemptive.

Chapter 8

MISCONCEPTIONS OF THE KINGDOM OF GOD
IN EARLY CHRISTIANITY

Introduction

One of the many themes discussed in the Hellenistic era was that of the 'ideal state' or utopia. Thus Aristotle gave attention to those who had promoted various viewpoints περὶ τῆς πολιτείας τῆς ἀρίστης[1] and sought to determine the best constitution for government. In his analysis, Aristotle subjected Plato's *Republic* to criticism and often rejected that model of the perfect society, even dismissing its fundamental assumptions as being in error.[2] Aristotle felt free to depart from the teachings of 'Socrates' although he recognized their implicit authority:

> While it is true that all the discourses of Socrates are brilliant, witty, innovative, and searching, it is clear that it is difficult to be correct about all things.[3]

As early Christianity wrestled with many of the descriptions of the kingdom of God and the so-called 'entrance requirements' of that eschatological dominion, it is evident that some revision and reinterpretation of the sayings attributed to Jesus was inevitable. This essay intends to explore the apparent attitude reflected in early Christian literature that some people had serious 'misconceptions' of the kingdom.

It is a common belief that when the angels announced the birth of the Christ child they indicated that his goal or mission was to bring 'peace on earth'.[4] It is significant that early Christian tradition itself apparently repudiates such a misunderstanding of his purpose.

---

1. Aristotle, *Politics* 1.5.12.
2. Cf. *Politics* 2.1.2, 17; 2.2.9; 5.10.1; 8.7.11.
3. *Politics* 2.3.3.
4. Cf. Lk. 2.14.

> Do not think that I have come to bring peace on earth; I have not come to bring peace, but a sword.[5]

This correction formula seems to echo the statement, 'Do not think that I have come to abolish the law and the prophets; I have not come to abolish them but to fulfil them.'[6] Another challenge to those who would misinterpret the intentions of Jesus is found in Mk 2.17—'...I came not to call the righteous, but sinners'.

These revisionist claims are related to several kingdom of God texts that implicitly or explicitly reject one view of kingdom standards in favour of another.[7] For example, Matthew again reports that Jesus said

> I tell you, many will come from east and west and eat with Abraham, Isaac, and Jacob in the kingdom of heaven, while the heirs of the kingdom will be thrown into the outer darkness, where there will be weeping and gnashing of teeth (Mt. 8.11-12).

This passage clearly warns that one can be disinherited from the kingdom. The danger exists that some will have misconceptions about the kingdom. This realization or fear prompts Paul to write

> Do you not know that the unrighteous will not inherit the kingdom of God? Do not be deceived; neither the immoral, nor idolators, nor adulterers, nor sexual perverts, nor thieves, nor the greedy, nor drunkards, nor revilers, nor robbers will inherit the kingdom of God (1 Cor. 6.9-10).

Within early Christian literature there are a number of indications that certain views of the kingdom of God were prevalent among Christians and that these views were rejected by others, dismissed as virtually heretical; thus Paul's remark 'Do not be deceived'.[8] This identical warning occurs elsewhere in two other kingdom passages that seek to correct a misconception.[9]

---

5. Mt. 10.34 cf. Lk. 12.51; *Gos. Thom.* 16.

6. Mt. 5.17. Reference can be made also to *2 Clem* 1.1-2 where the author may be 'correcting' another apparent misconception of Jesus.

7. Regarding a separate, but similar, issue, Ben Wiebe observes, '...different from that offered by any of Jesus' contemporaries...it is based on a different understanding of the kingdom': 'Messianic Ethics', *Int* 45 (1992), p. 34. Cf. also, P.J. Achtemeier, 'An Apocalyptic Shift in Early Christian Tradition', *CBQ* 45 (1983), pp. 231-48.

8. μὴ πλανᾶσθε.

9. Ignatius, *Eph.*16.1; *Phld.* 3.3; See also 1 Cor. 15.33; Gal. 6.7; Jas 1.16; 1 Jn 3.7; Rev. 20.3; Ignatius, *Magn.* 8.1; cf. Eph. 5.6. Perhaps this was, in part, a response to the accusation that Jesus himself was a 'deceiver' (Jn 7.47). More significant,

Some kingdom standards are regarded as astonishing, even mysterious.[10] This unexpectedness is in fact a rejection of accepted views of the kingdom and its entrance requirements. Similarly, regarding the anticipation of the kingdom's arrival, Luke claims that Jesus twice corrected the misconception of his followers that the kingdom was near.

> …he went on to tell a parable because he was near Jerusalem and because they supposed that the kingdom of God was to appear immediately (Lk. 19.11).

> So when they had come together they asked him, 'Lord, is this the time when you will restore the kingdom to Israel?' He replied, 'It is not for you to know the times or periods that the Father has set by his own authority' (Acts 1.6-7).

Luke even indicates that Jesus rejected the traditional expectation—which Christianity nevertheless came to hold—that the arrival of the kingdom of God would be 'announced' with certain apocalyptic indicators.

> Once he was asked by the Pharisees when the kingdom of God was coming, and he answered, 'The kingdom of God is not coming with things that can be observed; nor will they say, "Look, here it is!" or "There it is!" For, in fact, the kingdom of God is among you' (Lk. 17.20-21).

This context of various beliefs and interpretations provides the background for our concern with the attempts within early Christianity to correct what were thought to be mistaken perceptions of the kingdom of God.

Variant Appeals to the Sayings of Jesus

Many of the conflicts and divisions in the early church were due to differing attitudes towards and interpretations of the Hebrew scriptures. Radically divergent theologies and practices could find justification in the Law, the Prophets, and the Writings. The circumcision controversy in early Christianity is clear evidence of this.[11]

Another source of disagreement—or divided loyalty—in the early Christian community was the existence of various collections of the

---

however, is the close association with the eschatological warning/prediction that 'false Christs and false prophets will arise and show great signs and wonders, so as to lead astray (πλανῆσαι), if possible, even the elect' (Mt. 24.24//Mk 13.22).

   10. E.g., Mk 10.23-26; Jn 3.3-9; 1 Cor. 15.50-51.

   11. Cf. R. Meyer, 'περιτέμνω', *TDNT* 6 (1968), pp. 81-84.

sayings of Jesus. Where these supplemented the Hebrew scriptures—or even replaced them[12]—the potential for misunderstandings was aggravated by the inevitable questions relating to how the logia should be applied to new circumstances and problems.

There is suggestive evidence that these traditions of Jesus' sayings were known in the Hellenistic churches outside Palestine and were the subject of considerable 'discussion and interpretation'.[13] In particular, the Christian community at Corinth is thought to have known a collection of the words of Jesus that stressed themes and ideas that Paul felt needed to be modified and corrected.[14] In this connection Peter Richardson makes the observation that 'in many cases, when Paul is negating something he does so because it is part of the position he is countering'.[15] I will argue that there are in early Christian literature several 'negative' statements about the kingdom of God and that these seem to be in response to interpretations of traditions of the sayings of Jesus.

1 Corinthians

According to Acts, one of the themes of the preaching of the early Christians was the necessity of 'tribulations' (θλίψεων) as a virtual entrance requirement for the kingdom of God (14.22). This belief is echoed in 2 Thess. 1.5-6 and the Lukan portrait of Paul represents the kingdom of God as a central focus of the apostle's message (Acts 19.8; 20.25; 28.23, 31). However, in his extant correspondence with communities of Christians Paul only infrequently refers to the kingdom of God. Furthermore, in several of these passages Paul seems concerned to

---

12. Cf. the case of Marcion. See H. Chadwick, *The Early Church* (Harmondsworth: Penguin, 1967), pp. 38-40.

13. H. Koester, *Ancient Christian Gospels* (Philadelphia: Trinity, 1990), pp. 50-54.

14. Koester, *Ancient*, p. 55; P. Richardson, 'Gospel Traditions in the Church in Corinth', in G.F. Hawthorne and O. Betz (eds.) *Tradition and Interpretation in the New Testament* (Tubingen: Mohr, 1987), pp. 302-304. James M. Robinson made the statement, 'The Q material may be used to illustrate the kind of tradition the Corinthians could have speculated upon in developing their heresy': 'Basic Shifts in German Theology', *Int* 16 (1962), p. 82. Cf. D.L. Balch, 'Backgrounds of 1 Cor. VII: Sayings of the Lord in Q', *NTS* 18 (1972), p. 352.

15. P. Richardson, 'The Thunderbolt in Q and the Wise Man in Corinth', in P. Richardson and J.C. Hurd (eds.), *From Jesus to Paul* (Waterloo, Ont.: Wilfrid Laurier University Press, 1984), p. 102.

dispel what he regards as common misunderstandings of the kingdom. Rather than supporting the apparently widespread traditions, the apostle constantly challenges and refutes them.

In his first letter to the Corinthians, Paul repudiates a number of 'misconceptions' of faith and practice that characterize the community. Among his several 'corrections' is the insistence that love, not knowledge, ought to be the motive of Christian behaviour. Out of love, one must be willing to surrender all claims, all rights (cf. 6.7b). This, he maintains, should even shape the Christian's attitude towards food (8.1-3, 7-13; cf. 13.2). As Paul responds to the Corinthian problems, seeking to apply the principle of love, he makes some observations about the kingdom of God; in each case he apparently rejects a common (or prevalent) interpretation.

A second theme dominates 1 Corinthians. This is Paul's defence of his status as an apostle, one with authority in the church. It is with ironic humility that he says, 'I think that I have the Spirit of God' (7.40). Throughout the letter Paul responds to those who would challenge or question his 'credentials'; not only does he insist that he has a right to an apostle's privileges (a right that he chooses *not* to exercise, 9.1-18[16]) but he almost dares to say he is a superior apostle to the so-called twelve (15.10). By the time 2 Corinthians 10–12 is written, Paul barely restrains his boasting. But in 1 Corinthians he is responding to the early signs of 'disparagement'[17] from those in Corinth who do not accept his authority.

Both of these concerns provide insights into the background of Paul's statements about the kingdom of God in 1 Corinthians.

1 Corinthians 4.20

> For the kingdom of God is not in talk but in power.

This stark contrast between ἐν λόγῳ and ἐν δυνάμει is a clear echo of Paul's earlier claim: 'my talk (ὁ λόγος μου) and my message were not in plausible words (λόγοις) of wisdom but in demonstration of the Spirit and power' (δυνάμεως; 2.4; cf. 1 Thess. 1.5). This antithesis characterizes Paul's understanding of the proclamation of the cross as an expression

---

16. This is itself an example of Paul's conflict with the Jesus tradition known in Corinth. See D.L. Dungan, *The Sayings of Jesus in the Churches of Paul* (Oxford: Blackwell, 1971), pp. 3-40.

17. Cf. P. Lampe, 'Theological Wisdom and the "Word about the Cross"', *Int* 44 (1990), p. 117.

of God's power (and wisdom) that mocks human talk and the so-called knowledge and speculation of the worldly-wise (1.17-18). It is striking that Paul regards power as manifested in love and a gentle spirit (4.21).

At the same time Paul is challenging those who doubt his intention to visit Corinth in the near future. Paul writes with apparent contempt 'I will find out not the talk of these arrogant people but their power' (4.19).[18] He then insists that he is in fact applying a kingdom principle to the situation (4.20).

Paul may have had in mind some form of the tradition later reported in Mark: 'Truly I tell you, there are some standing here who will not taste death until they see that the kingdom of God has come in *power*' (9.1). The suggestion that the apostle was influenced by this saying is not outrageous; indeed, on another issue it seems to provide the basis for his claim in 1 Cor. 15.50ff:

> ...Flesh and blood cannot inherit the kingdom of God, nor does the perishable inherit the imperishable. Listen, I tell you[19] a mystery! *We will not all die*, but we will all be changed.

In 4.20 Paul is deliberately associating his ministry with the term 'power' in contrast to the term 'talk'. This same tension is reflected in 2 Cor. 10.10: 'For they [Paul's opponents] say "His letters are weighty and strong but his bodily presence is weak and his talk (λόγος) is of no account."' In responding to this criticism, Paul insists that his ministry, like the kingdom of God, is a model of power, not talk.

This perhaps assumes, however, that Paul was then rejecting a view of the kingdom that gave utterance or language special prominence. Did some early Christians—opponents of Paul?—actually regard 'talk' as a manifestation of the kingdom? How could such an interpretation of the kingdom find justification?

This essay maintains that such an interpretation did exist although Paul's blunt description 'the kingdom is talk' would be an oversimplification. The more apparent reference is to those who regarded theological eloquence and wisdom-laden rhetoric as evidence of the kingdom's presence and the Spirit's inspiration. These who claimed to be filled, even kings (1 Cor. 4.8), believed that the coming of the

---

18. Here Paul's defence is an eerie echo of Socrates' statement in Plato's *Apology* 32A,D: 'not words, but deeds' (οὐ λόγῳ ἀλλ' ἔργῳ).

19. Is the formula λέγω ὑμῖν significant or coincidental? In Mk 9.1 Jesus says ὑμῖν λέγω.

kingdom was demonstrated by their sophia-talk.[20]

The less apparent possibility, however, is that Paul considered glossolalia itself as mere talk and that he not only dismissed it as an inferior gift but felt that, in some ways, it was insignificant. On the one hand, the apostle insists that love was a greater gift than this 'talk' (cf. 13.1) which Paul implied was virtually infantile gibberish.[21] On the other hand, Paul wishes to assert his apostolic credentials, even as he minimizes the significance of the gift of glossolalia: 'I thank God that I speak in tongues more than you all; nevertheless, in church I would rather speak five words with my mind, in order to instruct others, than ten thousand words in a tongue' (14.18-19). Paul challenges the view that the kingdom was in some sense 'talk'. In correcting this misconception he reaffirms the priority of love (as a kingdom principle) and reasserts his own apostolic credentials. He claims that in love he willingly sets aside his rights, privileges, and even his use of gifts.

The opponents of Paul—those who exalted the gift of tongues, mocking Paul's lack of rhetorical wisdom, those who disparaged his authority—regarded the kingdom of God as, in some sense, ἐν λόγῳ, filling them with divine 'talk', even the tongues of angels.[22] Paul seeks to correct this misconception.

---

20. Again for the association between wisdom, eschatology, and a collection of Jesus' sayings known in Corinth see Richardson, 'Gospel Traditions' and Koester, *Ancient*, p. 60. Also note the observation echoed by many, 'The Corinthians were behaving as if they thought the kingdom of God had already fully come' (Craig, *1 Corinthians*, p. 55).

21. '...As for tongues they will cease... When I was a child I spoke like a child...when I became a man I gave up childish ways' (13.8-11; cf. 3.1).

22. Cf. the excellent article by D.B. Martin, 'Tongues of Angels and Other Status Indicators', *JAAR* 59 (1991), pp. 547-89. There are parallels between the ecstatic language of tongues and the 'inspired' utterances of the Greek poets. Might this be another source for understanding the glossolalia pride in Corinth?

> ...the Muse inspires mortals and then by means of these inspired persons the inspiration spreads to others...a poet...is unable ever to compose until he has been inspired and put out of his senses and his mind is no longer in him...(Plato, *Ion* 533E-534B-C).

That there would be some relationship between the inspired poets and the theological wise man is implied in Clay's comment: 'What distinguishes the Muses from other divinities is that they convey this superhuman knowledge to the poets...As a result, the poet is constantly a theologian, literally a *theologos*...': *The Wrath of Athena* (Princeton, NJ: Princeton University Press, 1983), pp. 20, 25.

1 Corinthians 6.9-10

> Do you not know that the unrighteous will not inherit the kingdom of God? Do not be deceived; neither the immoral, nor idolators, nor adulterers, nor sexual perverts, nor thieves, nor the greedy, nor drunkards, nor revilers, nor robbers will inherit the kingdom of God.[23]

The common reaction to these verses, to this ethical standard for inheriting the kingdom of God, is to consider it as obvious; of course only the righteous should inherit the kingdom of God.[24] This was certainly the accepted criterion of intertestamental Judaism and the early Christian community.[25]

Yet the warning 'do not be deceived'[26] surely indicates that the Corinthians had been exposed to, perhaps even persuaded by, another interpretation. It is reasonable to regard Paul as confronting and denouncing ('Don't you know?'[27]) the view that the unrighteous *would* inherit the kingdom of God. How could such a position, however, find support in early Christian tradition?

Inasmuch as the Corinthians, in embracing the possibility that the *un*righteous would inherit the kingdom, were overthrowing a long-established tradition and standard, it is essential to assume that they would do so only where a voice of authority sanctioned such a view. Whose authority could legitimate the idea that those guilty of sexual misconduct, robbery or greed could enter the kingdom of God?

Only the words of Jesus could account for the Corinthian 'misconception'.[28] And the sayings tradition—perhaps even Q itself—

23. Cf. Gal. 5.19-21; Eph. 5.5.

24. Paul's catalogue of vices in 1 Cor. 5.11 (of which 6.9-10 seems to be an echo) is generally regarded as a standard list of 'behaviours' that are inappropriate for Christians. See, for example, Conzelmann, *1 Corinthians*, pp. 100-101,106.

25. Cf. Mt. 5.20; Wis. 14.22-31. 'Christianity takes over the Jewish ethic... Christianity regards itself not as a new system of ethics, but as a practical exercise of the will of the long-known God': Conzelmann, *1 Corinthians*, p. 101.

26. Cf. Epictetus 2.20.7; 2.22.15; 4.6.23.

27. This phrase, prominent in 1 Cor. 6, implies that they *ought* to know. While it imitates conventional rhetorical usage, it taunts the Corinthians' boast of spiritual knowledge. 'Don't you know?' references include Epictetus 3.24.31; Dio Chrysostom, *Slavery and Freedom II* 17 and *On Servants* 10, 19; Plutarch, *Table Talk* 681D; Xenophon, *Memorabilia* 1.6.5 and *Symposium* 4.21; Cicero, *Paradoxa Stoicorum* 30.

28. Cf. M. Smith, 'Paul's Arguments as Evidence of the Christianity from which he Diverged', *HTR* 79 (1986), p. 256.

has preserved a striking logion that may explain their position which Paul opposes. It is important to note that in this letter the apostle felt free to 'depart' from other known 'words of the Lord' (1 Cor. 7.10-16; 9.14-15[29]):

> Truly I tell you,[30] the tax collectors and the prostitutes are going into the kingdom of God ahead of you (Mt. 21.31b).

This logion certainly implies that the unrighteous—the sexually immoral and the greedy and dishonest—will have priority in the inheritance of the kingdom. Surely such an understanding would promote the Corinthian 'misconception'. Paul rejects their interpretation, insisting that so-called Christians who live in an unholy manner should not even be welcomed at the common table (5.11). Although there are clear reasons for Paul's response, perhaps his Pharisaic instincts and heritage helped to shape his reaction (cf. Mk 2.15-16; Lk. 15.1-2).

1 Corinthians 15.50

> ...Flesh and blood cannot inherit the kingdom of God, nor does the perishable inherit the imperishable.

Here Paul challenges the belief that 'flesh and blood', mortal bodies, can enter into the kingdom without being changed, in some sense reclothed. Paul insists that 'neither the living nor the dead can take part in the Kingdom of God—as they are'.[31] It may be assumed that Paul is rejecting the view that the kingdom has already fully arrived. In announcing this correction, he indicates that he is making known a mystery (15.51). This unexpected message contradicts a common belief.

It may be asked, then, why some early Christians came to believe that such a change in their bodies was *not* necessary for entrance into the kingdom. We are concerned to find the background for the position that Paul dismisses.

A saying found in Mk 9.1[32] may have been the foundation text:

---

29. For an analysis of Paul's attitude towards these traditions, see Dungan, *Sayings of Jesus*.

30. The authority of Jesus is reinforced by the phrase ἀμὴν λέγω ὑμῖν; Jeremias, *New Testament Theology*, pp. 35-36.

31. J. Jeremias, '"Flesh and Blood Cannot Inherit the Kingdom of God"', *NTS* 2 (1955–56), pp. 152-53.

32. Thus the forceful irony that Paul and those with whom he disagrees use and interpret (in different ways) the same traditions. As Balch asked, 'Has Paul been

> Truly I tell you, there are some standing here who will not taste death until
> they see that the kingdom of God has come in power

This passage would account (in part) for the expectation that the kingdom of God would arrive in the lifetime of the first Christians[33] and probably provided support for the interpretation that those still living would inherit the kingdom as 'flesh and blood'. Paul not only regarded *power* as an important characteristic of the kingdom's presence but apparently understood the idea of 'not tasting death *until*' (ἕως) as referring to a necessary, radical transformation making those standing there ('those still alive'; cf. 1 Thess. 4.17) able to inherit the kingdom.

It surely is not a mere coincidence that two of the central logia which would legitimate the Corinthian 'misconceptions' of the kingdom of God were preserved in the tradition with the solemn introductory formula 'Truly I say to you' (Mt. 21.31b; Mk 9.1). This *amen* phrase, which stresses the authority of the words of Jesus, would sanction these interpretations. The following passage is enlightening in this context:

> The point of the Amen before Jesus' own sayings is rather to show that as such they are reliable and true, and that they are so as and because Jesus Himself in His Amen acknowledges them to be His own sayings and thus makes them valid. These sayings are of varied individual content, but they all have to do with the history of the kingdom of God bound up with His person.[34]

Confronting these Corinthian positions, Paul walked a fine line in asserting his own apostolic authority while challenging the authority of the words of the Lord. This explains his willingness to 'set aside' other traditions of the Lord's teaching (again cf. 7.10-16; 9.14-15).

Other Early Christian Texts

Romans 14.17

> For the kingdom of God is not food and drink but righteousness and peace and joy in the Holy Spirit.

---

forced to appeal to the same authority as his opponents were using?' ('Backgrounds of 1 Cor. VII', p. 356).

33. 'We will not all die', 1 Cor. 15.51.

34. H. Schlier, 'ἀμὴν', *TDNT*, I, p. 338.

Paul's concerns and objectives in his letter to the Roman Christians were quite different from those prompting the writing of 1 Corinthians.[35] While the apostle is certainly less familiar with the issues and problems facing the Roman congregation, still he addresses some specific needs of that community. In particular, ch. 14 gives attention to questions of conscience that apparently threatened to divide their fellowship, especially whether a Christian should eat only vegetables (14.1-2).

Almost echoing his comments in 1 Corinthians about the eating of so-called idol food,[36] Paul writes to the Romans,

> I know and am persuaded in the Lord Jesus that nothing is unclean in itself, but it is unclean for anyone who thinks it unclean. If your brother is injured by what you eat, you are no longer walking in love. Do not let what you eat cause the ruin of one for whom Christ died (Rom. 14.14-15).

In this context Paul seeks to 'correct' a Roman misconception of the kingdom of God as a matter of food *and drink*. The inclusion of the reference to 'drink' indicates that the apostle is not simply calling his readers to a more spiritual attitude towards food alone. Inasmuch as 'drink' has not been mentioned previously in ch. 14, it is at least worth considering that Paul confronts a common interpretation of the kingdom of God as involving more than food;[37] in some sense it is a matter of eating and drinking.

Once again the view Paul opposes has gained acceptance through the authority of Jesus. Paul grants that for Jesus all foods are clean.[38] Yet the apostle maintains that for the 'weak' some foods are unclean and this scruple must be honoured out of love. Those who held that the kingdom of God was food and drink would find further support for their view in the sayings tradition. Furthermore, these logia have been preserved in the Gospels with the sacred formula 'I tell you':

> I tell you, many will come from east and west and will eat with (cf. Luke: have table fellowship with, 13.29) Abraham, Isaac, and Jacob in the kingdom of heaven (Mt. 8.11).

---

35. For a recent study of Paul's intentions in writing Romans, see G. Smiga, 'Romans 12.1-2 and 15.30-32 and the Occasion of the Letter to the Romans', *CBQ* 53 (1991), pp. 257-73.

36. Cf. 1 Cor. 8.9-13; 10.23-29a.

37. Cf. Lk. 14.15.

38. Cf. Mk 7.19.

> I tell you, I will not eat [the Passover] until it is fulfilled in the kingdom of God…[F]rom now on I will not drink of the fruit of the vine until the kingdom of God comes (Lk. 22.16-18).

The reference to drinking from the fruit of the vine in the kingdom of God indicates that there was a conception of the kingdom as a virtual banquet table at which liquid refreshment would be enjoyed. This would account for Paul's statement, 'the kingdom of God is not food and *drink*', in a context where it is expected that he would specify food alone (cf. 1 Cor. 8.13).

The Roman conception of eating and drinking as experiences of the kingdom may account for the indulgence in 'partying' that Paul condemns. It is significant that his warning provides the virtual introduction to ch. 14:

> Let us then lay aside the works of darkness and put on the armor of light. Let us live honorably as in the day, not in reveling and drunkenness (μὴ κώμοις καὶ μέθαις)[39]

Ignatius Ephesians *16.1*

> Do not be deceived (μὴ πλανᾶσθε), my brothers, those who corrupt families (οἰκοφθόροι) will not inherit the kingdom of God.

Ignatius is concerned about the possibility that the Christians in the Ephesian community might be 'deceived'. While he seems confident that they have 'stopped their ears' (9.1) to the seductive influences of false doctrine, Ignatius nevertheless calls on the community not to be misled (cf. 5.2; 8.1).

Ignatius is aware that the Ephesians have been confronted by Christians who advocate a different tradition than the one he endorses; he characterizes them as those who 'make a practice of carrying the Name[40] with wicked guile' (7.1). To what teaching (διδαχήν, 9.1) had the Ephesians been exposed through these fellow-believers that Ignatius regarded as dangerous? Presumably it bore on questions of episcopal authority and the importance of corporate worship and the celebration of the Eucharist (cf. 2.2; 4.1; 5.1–6.2; 13.1-2). Yet for our purposes the most significant feature of their teaching may have encouraged a disregard for

---

39. These terms are closely associated with behaviour that is inappropriate for those who would enter the kingdom of God (cf. 1 Cor. 6.10 and Gal. 5.21). See Garrison, *Redemptive Almsgiving*, p. 126.

40. By 'the Name', Ignatius is referring to the name of the Lord. Cf. *Phld.* 10.1-2.

family. Ignatius warns his readers, 'Do not be deceived, my brothers, those who corrupt families will not inherit the kingdom of God' (16.1). He may well have understood this as a judgment on those who 'do this according to the flesh' and gone on to apply it to those who disrupt, or cause dissension within, the family of the church (16.2).[41]

If these teachers that Ignatius opposes had indeed advocated the view that true discipleship to Jesus necessitates a rejection of human family, they would have found clear support for their position in the sayings tradition, probably within Q itself:

> For I have come to set a man against his father and a daughter against her mother and a daughter-in-law against her mother-in-law. And a person's enemies will be members of one's own household (Mt. 10.35-36; cf. Lk. 12.53).

It is striking that the parallel of this logion in the *Gospel of Thomas* (16) ends with the word, 'and they will stand as solitaries' (μοναχός). If this saying was part of the tradition known to, and used by, the teachers Ignatius condemns, it is understandable why they would be reluctant (unwilling?) to participate in *corporate* worship (cf. 5.2-3).

Does the sayings tradition more explicitly indicate that those who disregard their families are not only true disciples but that they will in some sense inherit the kingdom of God? The logion preserved in Mk 10.29-30 would support this interpretation:

> Truly (ἀμὴν) I say to you, there is no one who has left house or brothers or sisters or mother or father or children or lands, for my sake and for the gospel, who will not receive a hundredfold now in this time, houses and brothers and sisters and mothers and children and lands [with persecutions] and in the age to come eternal life.

Those who brought a new tradition to Ephesus may have concluded that those who renounce their families for the Lord will inherit the kingdom in the age to come. Ignatius regards such an idea as monstrous and he warns the Ephesian Christians not to be deceived.

Ignatius Philadelphians *3.3*

> Do not be deceived (μὴ πλανᾶσθε), my brothers, if anyone follow a maker of schism (σχίζοντι) that person does not inherit the kingdom of God.

---

41. But Schoedel's view that Ignatius is referring to adultery does not really address the issue of deceptive teaching; *Ignatius of Antioch*, p. 79.

In writing to the church in Philadelphia, Ignatius is anxious to put an end to factions in the congregation which threaten its unity. When he had earlier visited the Christians in that community he had warned, by the Spirit's prompting, 'flee from divisions' (μερισμοὺς φεύγετε; 7.2). In his letter Ignatius virtually echoes this caution: 'flee from division' (φεύγετε τὸν μερισμὸν; 2.1).[42] Divisions result from 'bad teaching' (κακοδιδασκαλίας; 2.1) and this is also Ignatius's characterization of the doctrines in the Ephesian church (*Eph.* 16.2).

Ignatius identifies the source of this corrupting doctrine as tied to Judaism (6.1-2) but more specifically he indicates that the teachers were concerned to justify their beliefs on the 'archives (αρχείοις) in the gospel' (8.2). While this probably refers to the Hebrew scriptures,[43] these Jewish Christians were likely to have been aware of Jesus traditions that supported their views.

One such belief, regarded by Ignatius as deceptive, is the idea that a genuine follower of the Lord would actually encourage division, even schism. This would have found legitimacy in the sayings tradition. We return again to Lk. 12.51:

Do you think that I have come to bring peace on earth? No, I tell you (λέγω ὑμῖν), but rather division (διαμερισμόν).

Did Ignatius deliberately avoid using the term μερισμός in *Phld.* 3.3? If so, perhaps he knew that his opponents used a logion similar to the one found in Lk. 12.51 that may have employed the very word in order to justify their causing dissension. This possibility is not as remote as one might think. On the one hand, μερισμός is to be expected in the text;[44] on the other hand, Ignatius nowhere else uses any terms related in form to σχίσμα.

The Jewish Christians to whom Ignatius refers may well have believed that it was their responsibility in obedience to the words of the Lord to cause division. Furthermore, the tradition came to regard Jesus himself as a 'maker of schism' (Jn 7.43). Perhaps those who brought their message to Philadelphia sought to follow his example!

42. Schoedel, *Ignatius of Antioch*, p. 197.
43. Lightfoot, *The Apostolic Fathers*, II.2, pp. 270-71.
44. Cf. Schoedel, *Ignatius of Antioch*, p. 197.

Conclusion

As Aristotle sought to correct Socrates (Plato), Paul and Ignatius sought to modify what they regarded as serious misunderstandings of the kingdom of God among the Christians in Corinth, Rome, Ephesus, and Philadelphia even though many of these viewpoints were in fact grounded in the sayings tradition of Jesus' teaching. Paul in particular found it necessary to assert his own authority and delicately to challenge the words of the Lord. Ignatius, by contrast, simply regarded his opponents as enemies of the gospel of Christ.

Various 'misinterpretations' and 'corrections' are scattered across the history of the church. Often these are regarded as conflicting understandings of the biblical text but early Christian literature itself suggests that actually thecycle of misconception and response precedes the recognition of many of these documents as scripture.

Chapter 9

PAUL'S USE OF THE ATHLETE METAPHOR IN 1 CORINTHIANS 9*

Introduction

> When we see acrobats face without concern their difficult tasks and risk
> their very lives in performing them, turning somersaults over up-turned
> swords or walking ropes set at a great height or flying through the air like
> birds, where one misstep means death, all of which they do for a miser-
> ably small recompense, shall we not be ready to endure hardship for the
> sake of complete happiness? For surely there is no other end in becoming
> good than to become happy and to live happily for the remainder of our
> lives.[1]

The image of the athlete and the themes of training and competing were
familiar to the Graeco-Roman world of the first century CE. The Olympic
games were referred to, literally and metaphorically, as the supreme contest in which a person's natural or developed abilities and self-reliance[2]
were put to the test.[3] The works of Homer earlier employed this
symbolism.[4]

The symbolism is evident in the moral teachings of the Stoics and
Cynics.[5] The struggle against pleasure and pain is often described as an

* First published in *Studies in Religion/Sciences Religieuses* 22.2 (1993),
pp. 209-17. Thanks are due to the Canadian Corporation for Studies in Religion for
permission to reprint this article.

1. Musonius Rufus, from 'That One Should Disdain Hardships'. See Lutz,
'Musonius Rufus', p. 59. Cf. P.W. van der Horst, 'Musonius Rufus and the New
Testament', *NovT* 16 (1974), p. 311.

2. In the Olympics there was no team competition. All contests were between
individuals. Cf. M.I. Finley and H.W. Pleket, *The Olympic Games* (New York:
Viking Press, 1976), p. 22.

3. Cf. Philo, *Agr.* 119.

4. E.N. Gardiner, *Athletics of the Ancient World* (Chicago: Ares, 1980), pp. 1-
28.

5. And the imagery is perhaps most significant in Philo. See H.A. Harris,

ἀγών. It is claimed that they imitate 'their patron Hercules'.[6] The truly wise man is described as an athlete, expected to train for the Olympic competition of life itself:

> It is difficulties that show what men are. Consequently, when a difficulty befalls, remember that God, like a physical trainer, has matched you with a rugged young man. 'For what purpose?' someone will say. So that you may become an Olympic victor, but that cannot be done without sweat.

> The man who exercises himself against outward appearances is the true athlete in training… Great is the struggle, divine the task. The prize is a kingdom, freedom, serenity, peace. Remember God. Call upon him to help you and to stand by your side.

> God says to you, 'Give me proof that you have striven by the rules [cf. 2 Tim. 2.5], eaten what is prescribed, taken exercise, heeded your trainer.'

> Now God says to you, 'Come at last to the contest (τὸν ἀγῶνα) and show us what you have learned and how you have trained yourself. How long will you exercise alone? Now the time has come for you to discover whether you are one of the athletes who deserve victory or belong to the number of those who travel about the world and are everywhere defeated.'[7]

In exploring the letters of Paul and finding occasional comparisons between athletes and Christians in his work, we are 'confronted by a popular, traditional metaphor' where even 'a single term suffices to recall to mind the whole athletic image in its metaphorical use'. Alert to this significant background and context of the apostle's writings, we can recognize that several Pauline passages reflect 'a traditional use of the athletic image'.[8]

Especially in the light of the striking parallels between early Christianity and Cynicism,[9] it is not surprising to find Paul employing the symbol of the athlete in an exhortation similar to that of Musonius Rufus:

> Do you not know that in a race all the runners compete but only one receives the prize? So run that you may obtain it. Every athlete exercises self-control in all things. They do it to receive a perishable wreath, but we an imperishable (1 Cor. 9.24-26).

Greek Athletics and the Jews (Cardiff: University of Wales Press, 1976), p. 13; M.B. Poliakoff, *Combat Sports in the Ancient World* (New Haven, CT: Yale University Press, 1987), pp. 4, 143.

6.   V.C. Pfitzner, *Paul and the Agon Motif* (Leiden: Brill, 1967), pp. 1, 28.

7.   Epictetus, *Discourses* 1.24.1-2; 2.18.27-29; 3.10.8; 4.4.30.

8.   Pfitzner, *Agon*, p. 3.

9.   Cf. F.G. Downing, 'Cynics and Christians', *NTS* 30 (1984), pp. 584-93.

It is my purpose in this essay to probe Paul's use of the imagery of athletics. What is he trying to say? How does the symbolism enable him to communicate what cannot be said literally? What meaning would his first readers have found in the metaphor?

Themes in Paul's Use of the Metaphor

The Olympics, held every four years in Olympia, were the most famous athletic competition in the ancient world. The Isthmian games were a highly regarded panhellenic festival, celebrated every second year, featuring many of the same contestants. Corinth was the sponsor and approximate site of the latter ἀγών and 'the programme seems to have reflected in its variety the influence of that luxurious state'.[10]

Apparently the 'splendor and magnificence' of the Isthmian games were so well known that they provided a vivid background for Paul's athletic metaphor in 1 Corinthians.[11] It was further significant for the apostle that the athletes who competed in these contests had no desire (much less hope) simply to come third or even second; 'not to be first was to lose'.[12] Yet at Olympia the victor was only awarded an olive wreath and at the Isthmian games the prize was but a wreath of pine leaves.[13] The philosophical significance of this was implicit: the 'custom of rewarding the victor with no other prize than a wreath of leaves set an example of athletic purity which had an important influence on Greek athletics'.[14]

Indeed, the relative worthlessness of the wreath was conceded. It was the victory, the honour, that gave value to the wreath:

> Do you think these prizes are trivial? My dear fellow, it is not the bare gifts that we have in view! They are merely tokens of the victory and marks to identify the winners. But the reputation that goes with them is worth everything to the victors, and to attain it, even to be kicked, is nothing to men who seek to capture fame through hardships. Without the hardships it cannot be acquired. The man who covets it must put up with much unpleasantness in the beginning before at last he can expect the profitable and delightful outcome of his exertions.[15]

10. Gardiner, *Athletics*, pp. 36-37.
11. Gardiner, *Athletics*, p. 47. Cf. *2 Clem.* 7.1-3 and the interpretation in Lightfoot, *The Apostolic Fathers*, I.2, p. 223.
12. Finley and Pleket, *Olympic Games*, p. 22; cf. Lucian, *Anacharsis* 13.
13. Gardiner, *Athletics*, pp. 35-37.
14. Gardiner, *Athletics*, p. 36.
15. Lucian, *Anacharsis* 9-10.

Consequently, training and the rigorous demands of discipline required of the competitor were regarded as both necessary and beneficial. For the philosopher, 'the moral athlete must strictly follow his standards, just as the athlete must keep to his diet and prescribed exercises'.[16]

In addressing the Corinthians, Paul adopts the symbolism of the Isthmian games in order to call his readers to accept the full commitment of following Christ. His purpose, though distinctive, is similar to that of the Cynic and Stoic teachers who employ many of the same images:

> Do you not know that in a race all the runners compete, but only one receives the prize? So run that you may obtain it. Every athlete exercises self-control in all things. They do it to receive a perishable wreath, but we an imperishable (1 Cor. 9.24-26).

Two references in this passage warrant further attention: (1) self-control, and (2) the imperishable (wreath).

Self-control

Paul states, in proverb form, 'every athlete exercises self-control (ἐγκρατεύεται) in all things'. While the apostle uses this verb elsewhere to refer to mastery of the sexual appetite (1 Cor. 7.9),[17] the indication that the athlete's self-control is demonstrated in *all* things suggests that Paul here has in mind one of the broader spiritual virtues that characterizes the life of the mature Christian (cf. Gal. 5.22-23).[18]

It would seem that in 1 Cor. 9.25, self-control is closely related to αὐτάρκεια, the ability to adapt to all circumstances (cf. Phil. 4.11-13, also 1 Tim. 6.6), and Paul insists that the child of God is able to endure all conditions and be more than a victor (Rom. 8.35-37). Again a striking parallel may be found in the teachings of the Stoics:

16. Pfitzner, *Agon*, p. 32.

17. In *Laws* 839E-840A, Plato uses σωφρονεῖν in reference to a known athlete's control of the sexual urge (cf. Philostratus, *Life of Apollonius of Tyana* 1.13). But in 840C, Plato uses ἐγκρατεῖς to refer to general self-control. For the significance of this term being used interchangeably with ἐγκρατεύεται see below pp. 7-8. Cf. Plutarch, *Alexander* 21.5

18. Cf. C.K. Barrett, *The First Epistle to the Corinthians* (New York: Harper & Row, 1968), p. 217. Cf. Isocrates, *Demonicus* 21 for a moral application in a pre-Christian text.

Pfitzner's claim that 'In Paul such central hellenistic concepts as... ἐγκράτεια... play no part in his picture of the Christian Agon' seems untenable (*Agon*, p. 6). Cf. what he goes on to say on pp. 83, 87.

Who then is the invincible man? He whom nothing that is outside the sphere of his moral purpose can dismay. I consider the circumstances one by one, as I would do in the case of the athlete.

'This fellow has won the first round. What, then, will he do in the second? What if it be scorching hot? And what will he do at Olympia?'

It is the same way in the present case. If you put silver in a man's way, he will despise it. Yes, but what about a beautiful woman, or darkness, or the hope of glory? What about abuse or praise? Or death, what then? All these things he can overcome... The man who passes all these tests is what I mean by the invincible athlete.[19]

This 'victoriousness' was to characterize the life of the wise man who knowingly entered into the 'Olympic contest' of life where he would be trained and exercised by Zeus.[20]

It is not surprising to find that Socrates, who regarded self-control (ἐγκράτεια) as the 'foundation of all virtue', was considered to be the model of life, the one prepared for the ἀγών: 'I shall really endeavour both to live and, when death comes, to die as good a man as I possibly can be...and I invite you to share in this life and to enlist in this contest which I maintain excels all other contests.'[21]

The self-control of the athlete, and an undefeated champion at that, is perhaps best illustrated in the character of Melancomas. Dio Chrysostom reports that although this famous boxer was renowned for his physical attributes and achievements, 'he was even more remarkable for his self-control'.[22] This champion boxer was not beaten by any opponent nor by 'toil, heat, gluttony, or sensuality'. While Dio Chrysostom praises this athlete for σωφροσύνη (moderation or self-control), he acknowledges that ἐγκρατής is central to this virtue.[23] Significantly, those who mourn

---

19. Epictetus, *Discourses* 1.18.21-23.

20. Epictetus, *Discourses* 3.22.51, 102; cf. the character and teaching of Diogenes the Cynic in Diogenes Laertius 6.22, 34, 43, 70-71. Cf. also the 'crown' awarded to Titus for his act of self-control in Philostratus, *Life of Apollonius of Tyana* 6.29

21. Xenophon, *Memorabilia* 1.5.4; 1.2.1-2; 2.1.1; 1.2.14. On the claim that self-control is the foundation of virtue, cf. Philo's report about the Theraputae in *Vit. Cont.* 34. Cf. Philo, *Spec. Leg.* 1.173; Diogenes Laertius 2.24. See the so-called Cynic Epistle, *Crates to Metrocles* (#34 in Malherbe's edition, p. 86, line 1); Clement of Alexandria, *Strom.* 2.20; Plato, *Gorgias* 526D-E.

22. Dio Chrysostom, *Melancomas* 2.6; cf. *Melancomas* 1.8.

23. *Melancomas* 2.12; *Melancomas* 1.14. Cf. Philo, *Det. Pot. Ins.* 17-21. For the dual reference to self-control see also Musonius Rufus, 'Which is More Effective, Theory or Practice?' (Lutz, 'Musonius Refus', p.51). Cf. also *1 Clem.* 62.2.

the death of Melancomas are told, 'Bear your grief with self-control' (ἐγκρατής).[24]

How does this influence the interpretation of Paul's athletic metaphor in 1 Cor. 9.24-25? The apostle does not point to the example of a specific athlete as providing a pattern for Christian character or conduct. Instead, he encourages the imitation of the athlete in general, as one who runs, strives, and exercises self-control. And he recommends himself as a worthy model:

> I do not run aimlessly, I do not box as one beating the air. I pommel my body and subdue it, lest after preaching to others I myself should be disqualified (1 Cor. 9.26-27).

Paul regards himself as the athlete in training who is the appropriate example for the Corinthians.[25]

Significantly, Paul has been subjected to the harsh discipline of being an apostle. In this he has gained αὐτάρκεια and in the severe testing of his abilities he has conquered:

> To the present hour we hunger and thirst, we are ill-clad, buffeted, and homeless. We labor, working with our own hands. When reviled, we bless; when persecuted, we endure; and when slandered, we try to conciliate (1 Cor. 4.11-13).

Consequently, Paul is bold enough to offer himself as one who is worthy of imitation.[26] His own self-control is demonstrated in the willing, even eager, refusal to insist on his own rights and privileges and his voluntary sacrifice of his freedom (1 Cor. 9.1, 12, 15, 19; 2 Thess. 3.7-9).[27] What, then, would this mean for the Corinthians? How were they to imitate Paul's 'athletic' endurance, discipline and self-control?

The apostle's willingness to give up his own 'rights' for the sake of others provides an illustration of Christian love. It is the basis of his ethic regarding the eating of meat offered to idols.

---

24. *Melancomas* 1.22.
25. Cf. Conzelmann, *1 Corinthians*, pp. 161-62.
26. 1 Cor. 4.16; 11.1; Phil. 3.17; 4.9; cf. 2 Thess. 3.9.
27. Compare the analysis of F.F. Bruce: 'Self-discipline involves a voluntary curtailment of one's rights and liberties': F.F. Bruce, *1 and 2 Corinthians* (Grand Rapids, MI: Eerdmans, 1971), p. 89. It is worth noting here Pfitzner's observation concerning the 'self-apologetic character which underlies the most important Agon passages in the Pauline literature' (*Agon*, p. 11).

> If food is a cause of my brother's falling, I will never eat meat, lest I
> cause my brother to fall (1 Cor. 8.13).

While recognizing the theological superiority of the realization that 'we
are no worse off if we do not eat, and no better off if we do' (8.8), Paul
insists that *love*, not knowledge, must motivate the individual's action
(8.1). Paul regards this as the foundation of all behaviour that honours
God:

> So whether you eat or drink or whatever you do, do all to the glory of
> God. Give no offense to Jews or to Greeks or to the church of God, just
> as I try to please all men in everything I do, *not seeking my own*
> *advantage*, but that of many, that they may be saved. Be imitators of me
> as I am of Christ (1 Cor. 10.31–11.1).

Paul's references to surrendering his rights and not seeking his own
advantage (μὴ ζητῶν τὸ ἐμαυτοῦ σύμφορον) illustrate the character of
love. Just as he maintains that he 'endures all things' (πάντα στέγομεν,
1 Cor. 9.12b) for the gospel, so he describes love as 'not seeking its own
[advantage]...love endures all things' (οὐ ζητεῖ τὰ ἑαυτῆς...πάντα
στέγει, 13.5, 7). Thus Paul, in the exercise of self-control, exhibits the
virtue of Christian love. He is the example to be followed which is
recommended to the Corinthians.

The Imperishable Wreath
Paul contrasts the athlete's quest for a perishable crown with the
Christian's desire for a reward that is imperishable (ἄφθαρτον). This
parallelism is found in *2 Clem.* 7.1-3:

> So then my brothers, let us contend (ἀγωνισώμεθα), knowing that the
> contest is close at hand, and that many make voyages for perishable
> prizes, but not all are crowned, except those who have toiled hard and
> contended well. Let us so contend that we may all be crowned. Let us run
> the straight course, the immortal contest (ἀγῶνα τὸν ἄφθαρτον) and let
> many of us sail to it and contend that we may also receive the crown.

The symbolism of an indestructible prize, an abiding treasure, as the
future (i.e., after this life) reward of Christians is fairly common in early
Christian literature.[28] Indeed, the martyrdom of Polycarp was seen as his
means of gaining 'the crown of imperishability/immortality (ἀφθαρσίας
στέφανον)'.[29] Our concern here, however, is to focus on Paul's intention

---

28. E.g., Mt. 6.19-20; 2 Tim. 4.8; Jas 1.12; 1 Pet. 5.4; Rev. 2.10; 3.11.
29. *Mart. Pol.* 19.2.

and meaning. To what did the apostle refer when he wrote, 'They do it to receive a perishable wreath, but we an imperishable?' What, for Paul, was the imperishable crown for which he strived?

It is to be noted that Musonius encouraged the imitation of athletic discipline because such 'training' would yield happiness and virtue in the *present* life. This interest in the rewards for the wise person in the 'here and now' also characterizes the teachings of Epictetus: wisdom is its own prize.[30]

By contrast, early Christianity, and Paul in particular, seem to look ahead to an imperishable crown that will be received beyond the boundaries of the present, fading age (cf. 1 Cor. 7.29-31; 10.11). This is not to deny the apostle's immediate concern for ethical and spiritual development and maturity in the life of the Christian, but in 1 Cor. 9.24-26, it appears that his attention is focused on an 'otherworldly' crown.

Greek philosophy had long been intrigued by the question of immortality, 'of what abides in contrast to that which changes, which has a fixed span, which undergoes alteration in the world'. The term φθαρτόν 'is always defined by that of what abides and is immutable in the cosmos'.[31] In the first part of the fifth century BCE, Xenophanes had declared that 'everything which comes into being is doomed to perish'.[32] It was Plato, through the mouth of Socrates, who insisted that as opposed to the material world, God and the soul were undying, immortal.[33]

For Hellenistic Judaism, the immortality of the soul defined humanity's participation in the divine: 'God created humanity for "imperishability" (ἀφθαρσίᾳ) and made people in the image of his nature'.[34] Further, it was promised that the righteous would live forever (cf. Wis. Sol. 5.15).

The idea of resurrection 'clothes' the soul in eternity. For Paul, the resurrection of the body to an imperishable state was the dramatic fulfilment of the hope for immortality. Here the righteous, those 'in Christ', receive the imperishable reward of their faith and will bear the image of the heavenly one:

---

30. For Musonius, see quote on page 1. He concludes, '...surely *there is no other end* in becoming good than to become happy and to live happily for the remainder of our lives.' For Epictetus, see *Discourses* 3.24.52; 3.25.3; cf. 2.18.27-29.

31. G. Harder, 'φθείρω', *TDNT* 9 (1974), p. 95.

32. Diogenes Laertius 9.19.

33. Plato, *Phaedo* 105E-107A; 'nothing would escape destruction, if the immortal, which is everlasting, is perishable', 106D.

34. Wis. Sol. 2.23; cf. *4 Macc.* 17.10-16; 18.23.

Just as we have borne the image of the one of dust, we will also bear the image of the one from heaven. What I am saying, brothers, is this: flesh and blood cannot inherit the kingdom of God, nor does the perishable (ἡ φθορὰ) inherit the imperishable (ἀφθαρσίαν)....the dead will be raised imperishable (ἄφθαρτοι) and we will be changed. For this perishable body (φθαρτὸν) must put on imperishability (ἀφθαρσίαν); this mortal body must put on immortality (ἀθανασίαν).[35]

The 'imperishable crown' of 1 Cor. 9.26 is not a temporal reward: 'ἀφθαρσία is a strictly future blessing of salvation which is understood in exclusively eschatological terms'.[36]

There is further evidence to support this interpretation of the athlete metaphor. In writing to the Philippians, Paul speaks of the 'prize' for which he strives. Again there is the call to imitate his example and character and the promise of immortality is expressed in terms of resurrection, the transformation of 'perishable' flesh and blood:

...in order that I may gain Christ and be found in him, not having a righteousness of my own that comes through the law, but one that comes through faith in Christ, the righteousness from God based on faith. I want to know him and the power of his resurrection and the sharing of his sufferings by becoming like him in his death, if somehow I may attain the resurrection from the dead.

Not that I have already obtained this or have already been made perfect but I press on to make it my own, because Christ Jesus has made me his own. Brothers, I do not consider that I have made it my own but this one thing I do: forgetting what lies behind and straining forward to what lies ahead, I press on toward the goal for the prize of the upward call of God in Christ Jesus...

Join in imitating me and observe those who live according to the example you have in us...Our citizenship is in heaven and it is from there that we are expecting a Savior, the Lord, Jesus Christ. He will transform our humble bodies to be conformed to his glorious body (Phil. 3.8c-21a).

Conclusion

Paul's use of the athlete metaphor in 1 Cor. 9.24-26 echoes the themes and values of his contemporary culture. He employs the language and symbolism of other teachers of the first century CE (e.g., Philo, Musonius).

---

35. 1 Cor. 15.49-53. For a fascinating article on this passage, see Jeremias, '"Flesh and Blood Cannot Inherit the Kingdom of God"'.

36. Harder, 'φθείρω', p. 105.

For Paul, the purpose of the metaphor in its context is to call the Corinthians to the exercise of love demonstrated in self-control, an athletic self-denial of privilege and rights. He offers himself as the model worthy of imitation. In developing this imagery, Paul encourages his readers to pursue the 'imperishable crown'. This refers to the anticipated resurrection of the body and the hope of immortality promised to all who are found to be 'in Christ', living a life of faith and obedience. Such an interpretation is justified by the eschatological perspective of 1 Corinthians and is corroborated by the letter to the Philippians.

The athlete metaphor in 1 Cor. 9.24-26 enables Paul to communicate a challenge and goal that the Corinthians could understand because of similar moral imperatives from the Cynics and Stoics. This indicates that Paul himself was almost certainly influenced by this language picture. Still, the apostle seeks to make the image distinctively Christian.

BIBLIOGRAPHY

Achtemeier, P.J., 'An Apocalyptic Shift in Early Christian Tradition', *CBQ* 45 (1983), pp. 231-48.

Alexander, L., 'Luke's Preface in the Context of Greek Preface-Writing', *NovT* 28 (1986), pp. 48-74.

Armstrong, A.H., and R.A. Markus, *Christian Faith and Greek Philosophy* (New York: Sheed & Ward, 1960).

Aune, D.E., '*Septem Sapientium Convivium* (*Moralia* 146B-164D)', in H.D. Betz (ed.), *Plutarch's Ethical Writings and Early Christian Literature* (Leiden: Brill, 1978), pp. 51-105.

Balch, D.L., 'Backgrounds of 1 Cor. VII: Sayings of the Lord in Q', *NTS* 18 (1972), pp. 351-64.

Barrett, C.K., *The First Epistle to the Corinthians* (New York: Harper & Row, 1968).

Bartchy, S.S., 'Table Fellowship with Jesus and the "Lord's Meal" at Corinth', in R.J. Owens, Jr, and B.E. Hamm (eds.), *Increase in Learning* (Manhattan, KS: Manhattan Christian College, 1979), pp. 45-61.

Batey, R.A., 'Jesus and the Theatre', *NTS* 30 (1984), pp. 563-74.

Bergen, A.L.T., 'The Homeric Hymn to Aphrodite: Tradition and Rhetoric, Praise and Blame', *Classical Antiquity* 8 (1989), pp. 1-41.

Bickerman, E., *From Ezra to the Last of the Maccabees* (New York: Schocken Books, 1962).

Bowe, B.E., *A Church in Crisis* (Minneapolis, MN: Fortress Press, 1988).

Breytenbach, C., 'Zeus und der Leberdige Gott', *NTS* 39 (1993), pp. 396-413.

Bright, J., *Jeremiah* (AB, 21; Garden City, NY: Doubleday, 1965).

Brown, C.G., 'The Power of Aphrodite: *Bacchylides* 17, 10', *Mnemosyne* 44 (1991), pp. 327-35.

Brown, P., *The Body and Society* (New York: Columbia University Press, 1988).

Brown, R.E., *The Death of the Messiah* (2 vols.; New York: Doubleday, 1994).

Bruce, F.F., *1 and 2 Corinthians* (Grand Rapids, MI: Eerdmans, 1971).

—*1 and 2 Thessalonians* (Waco, TX: Word, 1982).

Burkert, W., 'Oriental Symposia: Contrasts and Parallels', in W.J. Slater (ed.), *Dining in a Classical Context* (Ann Arbor: University of Michigan, 1991), pp. 7-24.

Canterella, E., *Pandora's Daughters* (Baltimore, MD: Johns Hopkins University Press, 1987).

Case, S.J., *The Evolution of Early Christianity* (Chicago: University of Chicago Press, 1942).

—*Studies in Early Christianity* (New York: Century, 1928).

Chilton, B., *A Feast of Meanings* (Leiden: Brill, 1994).

Chadwick, H., *Early Christian Thought and the Classical Tradition* (Oxford: Oxford University Press, 1966).

—*The Early Church* (Harmondsworth: Penguin, 1967).

Clay, J.S., *The Wrath of Athena* (Princeton, NJ: Princeton University Press, 1983).

Conzelmann, H., *1 Corinthians* (Philadelphia: Fortress Press, 1975).

Cook, A.B., *Zeus* (New York: Biblo & Tannen, 1964).

Corley, K.E., 'Were the Women around Jesus really Prostitutes? Women in the Context of Greco-Roman Meals', in D.J. Lull (ed.), *SBL Seminar Papers* (Atlanta: Scholars Press, 1989), pp. 487-521.

Countryman, L.W., *Dirt, Greed and Sex* (Philadelphia: Fortress Press, 1988).

Craig, C.T., *1 Corinthians* (Interpreter's Bible, 10; New York: Abingdon, 1953).

Cranfield, C.E.B., *The Gospel according to Saint Mark* (Cambridge: Cambridge University Press, 1963).

Dahl, N.A., *Jesus in the Memory of the Early Church* (Minneapolis, MN: Augsburg, 1976).

Daniélou, J., *Gospel Message and Hellenistic Culture* (Philadelphia: Westminster, 1973).

Danker, F.W., 'Menander and the New Testament', *NTS* 10 (1964), pp. 365-68.

Deissman, A., *Light from the Ancient East* (New York: George H. Doran, 1927).

Dexter, M.R., *Whence the Goddesses* (New York: Pergamon, 1990).

Dodds, E.R., *Pagan and Christian in an Age of Anxiety* (Cambridge: Cambridge University Press, 1965).

Downing, F.G., '*A Bas les Aristos*: The Relevance of Higher Literature for the Understandings of the Earliest Christian Writings', *NovT* 30 (1988), pp. 212-30.

—'Cynics and Christians', *NTS* 30 (1984), pp. 584-93.

Dungan, D.L., *The Sayings of Jesus in the Churches of Paul* (Oxford: Blackwell, 1971).

Dunn, J.D.G., 'Jesus, Table-Fellowship, and Qumran', in J.H. Charlesworth (ed.), *Jesus and the Dead Sea Scrolls* (New York: Doubleday, 1992), pp. 181-208.

Emerton, J.K., 'The Religious Environment of Early Christianity', *HTR* 3 (1910), pp. 181-208.

Finley, M.I., and H.W. Pleket, *The Olympic Games* (New York: Viking, 1976).

Fiorenza, E.S., *In Memory of Her* (New York: Crossroad, 1989).

Fitzmyer, J.A., *The Gospel according to Luke I–IX* (AB, 28; Garden City, NY: Doubleday, 1981).

—*The Gospel according to Luke X–XXIV* (AB, 28A; Garden City, NY: Doubleday, 1985).

Foerster, W., 'κλῆρος', *TDNT*, III, pp. 758-69.

Forbes, C., 'Comparison, Self-Praise and Irony: Paul's Boasting and the Conventions of Hellenistic Rhetoric', *NTS* 32 (1986) pp. 1-30.

—'Early Christian Inspired Speech and Hellenistic Popular Religion', *NovT* 28 (1986), pp. 257-70.

Gardiner, E.N., *Athletics of the Ancient World* (Chicago: Ares, 1980).

Garrison, R., *Redemptive Almsgiving in Early Christianity* (JSNTSup, 77; Sheffield: JSOT Press, 1993).

Geley, F.D., *Titus* (Interpreter's Bible, 11; New York: Abingdon, 1955).

Glover, T.R., *The Conflict of Religions in the Early Roman Empire* (Boston: Beacon Press, 1909).

Goodspeed, E.J., *A History of Early Christian Literature* (Chicago: University of Chicago Press, 1966).

—*Paul* (Philadelphia: Winston, 1947).

Gorman, P., *Pythagoras* (London: Routledge & Kegan Paul, 1979).

Grant, F.C., *Roman Hellenism and the New Testament* (Edinburgh: Oliver & Boyd, 1962).

Grant, R.M. *Gods and the One God* (Philadelphia: Westminster, 1986).

—'Hellenistic Elements in 1 Corinthians', in A. Wikgren (ed.), *Early Christian Origins* (Chicago: Quadrangle Books, 1961), pp. 60-66.

Grant, R.M., and H.H. Graham, *The Apostolic Fathers* (New York: Thomas Nelson & Sons, 1965).

Graves, R., *The Greek Myths* (2 vols.; Harmondsworth: Penguin, 1990).

Grigson, G., *The Goddess of Love* (New York: Stein & Day, 1977).

Guthrie, W.K.C., *The Greeks and their Gods* (Boston: Beacon Press, 1951).

Hadas, M., and M. Smith, *Heroes and Gods* (New York: Harper & Row, 1956).

Hamilton, E., *Mythology* (Boston: Little, Brown, 1942).

Harder, G., 'φθείρω', *TDNT* 9 (1974), pp. 93-108.

Harris, H.A., *Greek Athletics and the Jews* (Cardiff: University of Wales Press, 1976).

Harrison, P.N., *Polycarp's Two Epistles to the Philippians* (Cambridge: Cambridge University Press, 1936).

Hatch, E., *The Influence of Greek Ideas on Christianity* (New York: Harper & Brothers, 1957).

Hengel, M., *Between Jesus and Paul* (Philadelphia: Fortress Press, 1983).

—*The Charismatic Leader and his Followers* (New York: Crossroad, 1981).

—*Crucifixion* (Philadelphia: Fortress Press, 1977).

—*Judaism and Hellenism* (Philadelphia: Fortress Press, 1974).

Howatson, M.C. (ed.), *The Oxford Companion to Classical Literature* (Oxford: Oxford University Press, 1989).

Hull, A., *Jesus in Bad Company* (New York: Avon, 1972).

Irwin, T., *Classical Thought* (Oxford: Oxford University Press, 1989).

Jaeger, W., *Early Christianity and Greek Paideia* (Cambridge: Belknap, 1961).

—'Paideia Christi', *ZNW* 50 (1959), pp. 1-14.

—*Paideia: The Ideals of Greek Culture* (3 vols.; Oxford: Blackwell, 1946).

Jeremias, J., *New Testament Theology* (London: SCM, 1975).

—*The Parables of Jesus* (New York: Charles Scribner's Sons, 2nd rev. edn, 1972)

—'Perikopen-Unstellungen bei Lukas', *NTS* 4 (1958), pp. 115-19.

—'"Flesh and Blood Cannot Inherit the Kingdom of God"', *NTS* 2 (1955–56), pp. 151-59.

Johnson, L.T., *Sharing Possessions* (Philadelphia: Fortress Press, 1980).

Jones, C.P., *Plutarch and Rome* (Oxford: Clarendon Press, 1971).

Karris, R.J., 'Luke 23.47 and the Lucan View of Jesus' Death', *JBL* 105 (1986), pp. 65-74.

Kinsley, D., *The Goddesses' Mirror* (Albany, NY: SUNY Press, 1989).

Knox, W.L., *Some Hellenistic Elements in Primitive Christianity* (London: Oxford University Press, 1944).

Koester, H., *Ancient Christian Gospels* (Philadelphia: Trinity, 1990).

Kovacs, D., 'Euripides *Hippolytus* 100 and the Meaning of the Prologue', *Classical Philology* 75 (1980), pp. 130-37.

Kraemer, R.S., *Her Share of the Blessings* (Oxford: Oxford University Press, 1992).

Kurz, W.S., 'Luke 22.14-38 and Greco-Roman and Biblical Farewell Addresses', *JBL* 104 (1985), pp. 251-68.

Ladd, G.E., *The Pattern of New Testament Truth* (Grand Rapids, MI: Eerdmans, 1968).

Lake, K. (ed.), *The Apostolic Fathers* (Cambridge, MA: Harvard University Presss, 1976).

Lampe, P., 'Theological Wisdom and the "Word about the Cross"', *Int* 44 (1990), pp. 117-31.

Lévy, I., *La Légende de Pythagore de Grèce en Palestine* (Paris: Bibliotheque de L'Ecole des Hautes Etudes, 1927).

Liebermann, S., *Hellenism in Jewish Palestine* (New York: Jewish Theological Seminary of America, 1962).

Lightfoot, J.B., *The Apostolic Fathers* (5 vols.; Grand Rapids, MI: Baker, 1981).

Lindars, B., *New Testament Apologetic* (Philadelphia: Westminster, 1961).

Lutz, C.E., 'Musonius Rufus, "The Roman Socrates"', *Yale Classical Studies* 10 (1947), pp. 3-147.

MacDonald, M.Y., 'Women Holy in Body and Spirit', *NTS* 36 (1990), pp. 161-81.

MacGregor, G.H.C., *Acts* (Interpreter's Bible, 9; New York: Abingdon, 1954).

Mack, B., *A Myth of Innocence* (Philadelphia: Fortress Press, 1988).

MacLachlan, B., 'Sacred Prostitution and Aphrodite', *SR* 21/22 (1992), pp. 145-62.

Malherbe, A.J., '*Me Genoito* in the Diatribe and Paul', *HTR* 73 (1980), pp. 231-40.

—*Paul and the Popular Philosophers* (Philadelphia: Fortress Press, 1989).

Marquardt, P., 'Hesiod's Ambiguous View of Women', *Classical Philology* 77 (1982), pp. 283-91.

Marshall, I.H., *Commentary on Luke* (Grand Rapids, MI: Eerdmans, 1978).

Martin, D.B., 'Tongues of Angels and Other Status Indicators', *JAAR* 59 (1991), pp. 547-89.

Martin, J., *Symposion: Die Geschichte einer literarischen Form* (Paderborn: Schoningh, 1931).

Matera, F., 'The Death of Jesus according to Luke', *CBQ* 47 (1985), pp. 469-85.

—*What Are They Saying about Mark?* (New York: Paulist, 1987).

McGiffert, A.C., *The God of the Early Christians* (New York: Charles Scribner's Sons,, 1924).

Meeks, W.A., *The Moral World of the First Christians* (Philadelphia: Westminster, 1986).

—*The Origins of Christian Morality* (New Haven, CT: Yale University Press, 1993).

Meeus, X. de, 'Composition de Lc XIV et Genre Symposiaque', *ETL* 37 (1961), pp. 847-70.

Meyer, R., 'περιτεμνω', *TDNT* 6 (1968), pp. 72-84.

Milburn, R.L.P., *Early Christian Interpretations of History* (New York: Harper & Brothers, 1954).

Minn, H.R., 'Classical Reminiscence in St Paul', *Prudentia* 6 (1974), pp. 93-98.

Most, G.W., '"A Cock for Asclepius"', *Classical Quarterly* 43 (1993), pp. 98-99.

Moxnes, H., 'The Social Context of Luke's Community', *Int* 48 (1994), pp. 379-89.

Murphy-O'Connor, J., *St Paul's Corinth* (Wilmington, DE: Glazier, 1983).

Neusner, J., *From Politics to Piety* (Englewood Cliffs, NJ: Prentice Hall, 1973).

Neyrey, J.H. (ed.), *The Social World of Luke–Acts* (Peabody, MA: Hendrickson, 1991).

Nock, A.D., *St Paul* (New York: Harper & Row, 1963).

Nygren, A., *Agape and Eros* (trans. P. Watson; Philadelphia: Westminster, 1953).

O'Neill, J.C., 'The Lost Written Records of Jesus' Words and Deeds behind Our Records', *JTS* 42 (1991), pp. 483-504.

Orr, W.F., and J.A. Walther, *1 Corinthians* (AB, 32; Garden City, NY: Doubleday, 1976).

Patterson, L.G., *God and History in Early Christian Thought* (New York: Seabury, 1967).

Paul, G., 'Symposia and Deipna in Plutarch's *Lives* and in Other Historical Writings', in W.J. Slater (ed.), *Dining in a Classical Context* (Ann Arbor: University of Michigan, 1991), pp. 157-69.

Pearson, A.C., *The Fragments of Sophocles* (Cambridge: Cambridge University Press, 1917).

Pelikan, J., *Christianity and Classical Culture* (New Haven, CT: Yale University Press, 1993).

Pfitzner, V., *Paul and the Agon Motif* (Leiden: Brill, 1967).

Poliakoff, M.B., *Combat Sports in the Ancient World* (New Haven, CT: Yale University Press, 1987).

Powell, J.E., 'Father, into Thy Hands', *JTS* 40 (1989), pp. 95-96.

Quast, K., *Reading the Corinthian Correspondence* (New York: Paulist, 1994).

Quispel, G., 'God is Eros', in W.R. Schoedel and R.L. Wilken (eds.), *Early Christian Literature and the Classical Intellectual Tradition* (Paris: Editions Beauchesnes, 1979), pp. 189-205.

Renehan, R., 'Classical Greek Quotations in the New Testament', in D. Neiman and M. Schatkin (eds.), *The Heritage of the Early Church* (Rome: Pontificium Institutum Studiorum Orientalium, 1973), pp. 17-46.

Rhoads, D., and D. Michie, *Mark as Story* (Philadelphia: Fortress Press, 1982).

Richardson, P., 'Gospel Traditions in the Church in Corinth', in G.F. Hawthorne and O. Betz (eds.), *Tradition and Interpretation in the New Testament* (Tubingen: Mohr, 1987), pp. 301-18.

—'The Thunderbolt in Q and the Wise Man in Corinth', in P. Richardson and J.C. Hurd (eds.), *From Jesus to Paul* (Waterloo, Ont.: Wilfrid Laurier University Press, 1984), pp. 91-111.

Robbins, V.K., 'Prefaces in Greco-Roman Biography and Luke–Acts', *PerRS* 6 (1979), pp. 94-108.

Robinson, J.M., 'Basic Shifts in German Theology', *Int* 16 (1962), pp. 76-97.

Robertson, A.T., *Studies in Mark's Gospel* (ed. H.F Peacock; Nashville: Broadman Press, 1958).

Russell, D.S., *The Jews from Alexander to Herod* (Oxford: Oxford University Press, 1967).

Sandmel, S., 'Parallelomania', *JBL* 81 (1962), pp. 1-13.

Schlier, H., 'ἀμήν', *TDNT*, I, pp. 335-38.

Schmidt, K.L., 'ὁρίζω', *TDNT*, V, pp. 452-56.

Schoedel, W.R., *Ignatius of Antioch* (Philadelphia: Fortress Press, 1985).

Schoedel, W.R., and R.L. Wilken (eds.), *Early Christian Literature and the Classical Intellectual Tradition* (Paris: Editions Beauschesnes, 1979).

Scholer, D.M., and P.C. Finney (eds.), *The Early Church and Greco-Roman Thought* (New York: Garland, 1993).

Scodel, R., *Sophocles* (Boston: Harvard University Press, 1984).

Scott, E.F., 'The Limitations of the Historical Method', in S.J. Case (ed.), *Studies in Early Christianity* (New York: Century, 1928), pp. 3-18.

Scott, J.A., *Homer and his Influence* (New York: Cooper Square, 1963).

Scroggs, R., 'The Earliest Hellenistic Christianity', in J. Neusner (ed.), *Religions in Antiquity* (Leiden: Brill, 1968), pp. 176-206.

Seeley, D., *The Noble Death* (JSNTSup, 28; Sheffield: JSOT Press, 1990).

Shero, L.R., 'The *Cena* in Roman Satire', *CPh* 18 (1923).

Slater, W.J. (ed.), *Dining in a Classical Context* (Ann Arbor: University of Michigan, 1991).

Smiga, G., 'Romans 12.1-2 and 15.30-32 and the Occasion of the Letter to the Romans', *CBQ* 53 (1991), pp. 257-73.

Smith, D.E., 'Social Obligation in the Context of Communal Meals' (ThD dissertation, Harvard Divinity School, 1980).

—'Table Fellowship as a Literary Motif in the Gospel of Luke', *JBL* 106 (1987), pp. 613-38.

Smith, M., 'Palestinian Judaism in the First Century', in M. Davis (ed.), *Israel: Its Role in Civilization* (New York: Arno, 1956), pp. 67-81.

—'Paul's Arguments as Evidence of the Christianity from which he Diverged', *HTR* 79 (1986), pp. 254-60.

Soards, M.L., *The Passion according to Luke* (JSNTSup, 14; Sheffield: JSOT Press, 1987).

Soren, D., and J. Jones, *Kourion* (New York: Doubleday, 1988).

Stagg, E., and F. Stagg, *Woman in the World of Jesus* (Philadelphia: Westminster, 1978).

Stahlin, G., 'φιλέω', *TDNT* 9 (1974), pp. 113-46.

Stambaugh, J.E., and D.L. Balch, *The New Testament in its Social Environment* (Philadelphia: Westminster, 1986).

Stanton, G.N., *The Gospels and Jesus* (Oxford: Oxford University Press, 1989).

Steele, E.S., 'Luke 11.37-54—A Modified Hellenistic Symposium?', *JBL* 103 (1984), pp. 379-94.

Strathman, H., 'πόλις', *TDNT* 6 (1968), pp. 516-35.

Taylor, V., *The Gospel according to St Mark* (London: Macmillan, 1955).

—*The Passion Narrative of St Luke* (ed. O.E. Evans; Cambridge: Cambridge University Press, 1972).

Tcherikover, V., *Hellenistic Civilization and the Jews* (Philadelphia: Jewish Publication Society of America, 1959).

Thrall, M.E., *The First and Second Letters of Paul to the Corinthians* (Cambridge: Cambridge University Press, 1965).

Van den Brock, R. *The Myth of the Phoenix* (Leiden: Brill, 1972).

Van der Horst, P.W., 'Musonius Rufus and the New Testament', *NovT* 16 (1974), pp. 306-15.

—'The Unknown God (Acts 17.23)', in R. Von Den Broek, T. Baarda and J. Mansfeld (eds.), *Knowledge of God in the Graeco-Roman World* (Leiden: Brill, 1988), pp. 19-42.

Vernant, J.-P., *The Origins of Greek Thought* (Ithaca, NY: Cornell University Press, 1982).

Walaskay, P.W., 'The Trial and Death of Jesus in the Gospel of Luke', *JBL* 94 (1975), pp. 81-93.

Wardman, A., *Plutarch's Lives* (Berkeley, CA: University of California Press, 1974).

Weeden, T.J., *Mark—Traditions in Conflict* (Philadelphia: Fortress Press, 1971).

Wiebe, B., 'Messianic Ethics', *Int* 45 (1991), pp. 29-42.

Wilson, W.R., *The Execution of Jesus* (New York: Charles Scribner's Sons, 1970).

Woolf, B.L., *The Background and Beginnings of the Gospel Story* (London: Ivor Nicholson & Watson, 1935).

Wyatt, W.F., 'Sappho and Aphrodite', *Classical Philology* 69 (1975), pp. 213-14.

Yarbrough, O.L., *Not Like the Gentiles* (Atlanta: Scholars Press, 1985).

Yerkes, R.K., *Sacrifice in Greek and Roman Religions and Early Judaism* (New York: Charles Scribner's Sons, 1952).

Young, F.M., *Sacrifice and the Death of Christ* (London: SPCK, 1975).

INDEXES

INDEX OF REFERENCES

OLD TESTAMENT

NEW TESTAMENT

OTHER ANCIENT SOURCES

INDEX OF AUTHORS

JOURNAL FOR THE STUDY OF THE NEW TESTAMENT
SUPPLEMENT SERIES